10646787

DISCARD

ART CENTER COLLEGE OF DESIGN LIBRARY
1700 LIDA STREET
PASADENA, CALIFORNIA 91103

ART CENTER COLLEGE OF DESIGN

3 3220 00082 5195

TOPIARY

ART CENTER COLLEGE OF DESIGN LIBRARY
1700 LIDA STREET
PASADENA, CALIFORNIA 91103

715.1
C635

A. M. CLEVELY

TOPIARY

THE ART OF CLIPPING TREES AND ORNAMENTAL HEDGES

ART CENTER COLLEGE OF DESIGN LIBRARY
1700 LIDA STREET
PASADENA, CALIFORNIA 91103

Salem House Publishers
Topsfield,
Massachusetts

To the memory of Charles Samways ('Sam'), 1889–1980:
bookseller, author, gardener and friend

First published in the United States 1988 by
Salem House Publishers
462 Boston Street
Topsfield, MA 01983

Designed and produced by
Johnson Editions Ltd
15 Grafton Square
London SW4 0DQ, UK

Editor: Georgina Harding
Art director: Clare Finlaison
Picture research: Helena Beaufoy
Artwork: Paul Kime
Indexer: Richard Bird

© copyright A. M. Clevely 1988

Library of Congress Cataloging-in-Publication Data

Clevely, A. M., 1945–
    Topiary, the art of clipping
    trees and ornamental hedges.

    Includes index.
    1. Topiary work.   2. Topiary work–History.
    I. Title.
    SB462.C57 1988 715'.1 87-16564
    ISBN 0-88162-309-1

Typeset by Fowler Printing Services
Origination: Fotographics London/Hong Kong
Printed and bound in Hong Kong by Mandarin Offset Marketing (H.K.) Ltd.

Illustration on title page:
Topiary at Levens Hall, Cumbria.

CONTENTS

INTRODUCTION

There is a fascinating and timeless quality about topiary, whether it is the balanced pattern of hedges, cones and spirals in a stately formal garden, or a pair of yew doves guarding the gateway in front of a cottage. We usually expect to see topiary in such traditional surroundings, as a relic from a leisurely elegant age of wealthy estate-owners with craftsmen gardeners who could wield shears far more deftly than we use electric hedge-trimmers.

Complex as it looks, the principles of topiary are in fact the same as those used for simple hedge-trimming. It requires a little more planning beforehand, with perhaps the use of guides and formers, and an accidental slip of the shears may take longer to rectify; but there is no reason why amateur gardeners should not embark on topiary as confidently as they set about clipping privet hedges into straight lines every month in the summer.

Since the days of Ancient Rome, topiary has been an important form of garden decoration, employed in much the same way as stone statues — and in modern gardens, even gnomes. Over the centuries topiary has had varying fortunes in the great gardens and estates of the wealthy, whose interest sometimes exploded into mania only to decline equally abruptly into indifference, but it has always held a fascination for ordinary gardeners to the extent of becoming almost a folk art. In the past, it was part of the repertoire of skills possessed by gardeners in private service, and inevitably they reproduced some of their work in their own gardens, at first probably imitating the pheasants and peacocks or classical abstract shapes their employers favoured. From these beginnings the topiary cats, pigeons, jugs and armchairs of cottage gardens were natural home-made developments.

Today topiary in all its forms, from simple classical pyramids to grotesque animals and fat teddy-bears, can be seen in every kind of garden. A wide variety of plants is used, too. Yew and box are traditional for grand designs, but privet has often been employed, very successfully, by amateur gardeners because, as well as being so commonly found in small gardens, it is

Previous page: Trim hedges and specimen topiary give form and emphasis to beds of loose-growing foliage plants.

easily clipped into detail or trained on wires like ivy, and grows quickly into the finished shape. (Familiarity has bred fashionable contempt for the ubiquitous privet; perhaps one welcome result of the growing interest in topiary today might be the plant's overdue rehabilitation for ornamental hedging, in place of the dull Leyland cypress, whose monotonous rows never seem quite to blend with the rest of the garden.)

Shrubs such as cotoneaster, pyracantha and evergreen azaleas stand clipping into neat hedges, while fascinating designs can be traced on house walls with espaliers, the extra protection these situations provide allowing the use of such less hardy plants as camellias, fremontia, and even kumquats in a very sheltered courtyard. It is doubtful whether anyone has explored the full range of plants that will stand clipping or training into some ornamental form or other. A selection of the more reliable species is listed at the end of the book, but gardeners with very favoured sites or a sense of adventure could profitably experiment with countless others. Training fruit trees and bushes into numerous decorative shapes is another area of topiary, formerly more popular in large kitchen gardens and still practised by French gardeners; limited space has unfortunately prevented fuller treatment of the art in this book.

Just as there are many more plants suitable for topiary than most gardeners realize, so there are more techniques and shapes: topiary is not confined to aristocratic game birds carved out of yew. The origins of the word itself once implied a wider range of activities than is commonly meant these days. The term first appeared in Latin expressions used by Roman writers such as Pliny when he referred for example to the work of the ornamental gardener, 'in picturas operi topiarii', where the *topiarius* was the man who concentrated on pictures or special effects. Later, topiary was a description applied to any tree or shrub shaped by cutting or clipping, a narrower meaning than the Latin original but still more embracing than its modern usage.

According to that early description, front-garden hedges, pruned fruit trees, a dog cut in box and a wall-trained climbing rose are all examples of topiary. In this book topiary has been taken to mean the art of clipping (and training where also necessary) shrubs, trees and hedges into shapes that are decorative for their own sake, and therefore excludes pruning carried out purely for cultural reasons. Even so it remains a wide and varied field of activity that offers the gardener unusual scope for self-expression.

Of course there have been, and still are, those gardeners who argue against clipping plants into artificial shapes. Eighteenth- and nineteenth-century literature of reaction against earlier topiary excesses is full of such phrases as 'grotesque forms', 'fantastical operations' and 'quaint antagonism to Nature'. Topiary is undeniably an unnatural art; so is gardening as a whole. Almost every branch of horticulture involves cutting, restricting, selecting or forcing plants into behaviour quite foreign to their nature, and topiary is no exception. To argue against this is to revive the sentimental objections of the landscape movement which aimed to make gardens resemble a countryside totally untouched by man, ironically by interfering with nature on the grandest scale possible. Any form of gardening interferes with nature, and as one nineteenth-century writer retorted, 'it is no more unnatural to clip a yew-tree than to cut grass.'

Nor is it true to suggest that topiary belongs only in formal gardens and would be out of place in the 'wild gardens' popular today. This sounds a little like the cry of the lazy gardener whose wild garden is merely an excuse for untidiness and a dislike of weeding: even such a wilderness requires a boundary of some kind, usually a hedge, to enclose and define it, and to separate it from neighbouring gardens. The wildest painting needs a frame. And although historically typical of formal gardens, topiary need not always be formal, as countless cheerfully relaxed cottage gardens demonstrate. In fact, with sensitive choice of design, topiary can blend into virtually any garden style.

Moreover, the techniques involved can be tackled by anyone able to trim a hedge or prune a shrub to shape with secateurs (hand pruners). The mystique of an ancient and closely guarded craft, which seems to surround mature specimens in old gardens, is imaginary. Care and sharp tools are more essential than above-average dexterity and mistakes will grow out, given time.

Topiary does require patience, though not as much as some might suspect. Certainly it will not provide instant results, but nor will most of the worthwhile garden skills. Training a specimen figure can take five, ten, even fifteen years, depending on size and species, but that is no longer than many shrubs and most trees need before they look well established. Only a few hours' attention each season is required to develop the shape, which after ten years could appear to have been there for decades. With very little maintenance they will last that long, and more: some examples still vigorous today are well over 200 years old.

These days the most innovative topiary is often produced by amateur gardeners, who not only enjoy the mechanics of the craft but retain the flamboyance to design shapes with individuality and eccentricity. Once, not so long ago, showmanship was an essential ingredient of every trained gardener's character. Achieving the earliest peas, longest parsnips and biggest dahlias was a matter of pride, and a nicely turned piece of topiary was just one more flourish of his extrovert skill. But among professionals today, garden design often seems to be inhibited by a modern self-consciousness or excess of theory, a misplaced wariness of anything that might possibly be considered vulgar.

Nearly a hundred years ago topiary found a champion in John Sedding, who wrote in his book *Garden-craft Old and New*:

> I have no more scruple in using the scissors upon tree or shrub, where trimness is desirable, than I have in mowing the turf of the lawn that once represented a virgin world... And I would even introduce *bizarreries* on the principle of not leaving all that is wild and odd to Nature outside of the garden-paling; and in the formal part of the garden my yews should take the shape of pyramids or peacocks or cocked hats or ramping lions in Lincoln-green, or any other conceit I had a mind to, which vegetable sculpture can take.

An increasing number of gardeners today would share Sedding's uninhibited enthusiasm for topiary; it is hoped that after reading this book many more will agree with them.

A BRIEF HISTORY

ORIGINS

The definitive history of topiary has yet to be written. Brief accounts that do exist tend to concentrate on its development since the early seventeenth century, on a grand tradition well documented in contemporary works and engravings, and still witnessed in a few surviving historic gardens. For the seventeenth century had seen the beginning of the so-called Golden Age of topiary, when enthusiasm for clipped evergreens in every conceivable shape transformed topiary from a formal, almost architectural, feature — the role it had played in the medieval and Renaissance garden — into unrestrained garden sculpture.

But this was not the first time that gardeners had been beguiled by the remarkable adaptability of certain shrubs and trees in withstanding trimming into bizarre shapes; centuries earlier, wealthy Romans, too, had been as scissor-happy, populating their villa gardens with green menageries of wild and mythical animals. There are many contemporary descriptions of the Roman weakness for figurative topiary, and it is customary to regard these as marking its origins. Indeed, one Roman writer, Pliny the Elder, goes so far as to ascribe the 'discovery' of the method of cutting trees into regular shapes to Gnaius Mattius, a friend of Augustus. This would place the first appearance of topiary some time between 38BC, when the Emperor was born, and his death in 14AD.

Mattius, however, was a heroic poet and writer of popular farces. Even though we must assume his great interest in the work — he is also credited with inventing various techniques of propagation — he was certainly not a gardener as we understand the term. Gardening then, as now, was a manual occupation, below the dignity of a noble Roman. Although Columella, writing at the time of Augustus about the joys of digging and cultivation, often implies that he does the work himself, he is probably using literary licence — not the last writer in the history of gardening to give that impression while directing others to do the hard work.

In a sixteenth-century Italian parterre garden at Villa Lante, Bagnaia, swirling box hedges are set around the erect forms of clipped cypresses.

In Roman gardens this work was done by slaves. Several were likely to be employed in large villa gardens, which during the reign of Augustus had already become recognized symbols of the wealth of the ruling class. By division of labour each slave was entrusted with a different responsibility. One was given charge of the ornamental garden (*topia*) and he became known as *topiarius*, a landscape gardener or garden designer, at that time a workman rather than the desk-bound planner he has become.

In other areas of daily life foreign slaves are known to have introduced to the Romans customs and ideas from their own lands, and it is a fair assumption that captives from Roman campaigns abroad sold to work as slaves in villa gardens might have brought with them experience of rudimentary topiary. Some historians think the gardeners may have been Syrian or Jewish captives, others suggest Egyptian or Greek. It seems likely that trimmed hedges at least had long been a feature of the gardens of earlier Mediterranean and Asiatic cultures — first attempts at topiary probably motivated simply by a need to turn a rough row of sprawling plants into something more fitting for the gardens of rulers and nobles, and perhaps by the realization that cutting off the long shoots of shrubs regularly produces a denser, more impenetrable barrier against dry winds and hot sunshine. Here lies a challenge for anyone attempting a comprehensive history. Patient detective work will be needed because no unambiguous documentary evidence appears to record an earlier tradition of the craft, although tantalizing hints do occur.

When, for example, the Greeks marched under Alexander into the heart of the Persian empire, they found mature and splendid gardens that are known to have included hedges of clipped myrtle, and screens of plane, cypress and pines 'entangling their branches', perhaps a form of pleaching. In Egypt, too, the Greeks discovered a sophisticated culture with elaborate formal gardens and a love of decorative flowers (and considerable respect for the trade of the gardener) that astonished the invaders, who hitherto had been accustomed to gardens that were a combination of smallholding and private sacred wilderness.

In due course, in the process by which customs and skills are transmitted across cultures by conquest and trade, ideas brought back by the returning Greeks were adopted in turn by their successors, the Romans. The earliest records of Roman gardens that include detailed references to their topiary are letters written by Pliny the Younger sometime around 100AD in which he describes his two country villas. One of them, on the Italian coast near Ostia, contained formal clipped hedges of rosemary and box, but it was at his other residence in the foothills of the Appenines in Tuscany that he kept a lavish, though for the time presumably not unusual, collection of figurative topiary.

He wrote of 'a terrace, enclosed by a box hedge decorated with various shapes, from which a slope leads between facing pairs of animals cut from box'. Elsewhere in the garden are more box trees 'cut into thousands of different forms, some as letters spelling the name of the gardener or his master'. It is interesting to note that the *topiarius* himself is allowed to be immortalized in this way.

Earlier the writer's uncle, Pliny the Elder, included in his *Historia naturalis* a full description of the Mediterranean cypress (*Cupressus sempervirens*), an ancient species still much used in the region. At the time he was writing, about 70AD, he noted that the cypress was not only planted to form screens in vineyards, 'but nowadays is clipped or rounded off to a slender outline, and even used in the landscape gardener's art to make representations of hunting scenes, fleets of ships and imitations of real objects'.

The gardens of the Ancient Egyptians reflected the same formal aesthetic as their art. This papyrus, from 1340–1300BC, shows a symmetrical arrangement of palms and conical trees.

By all accounts the shaping of box and cypress trees seems already to have matured into a popular and almost excessively ornate gardening skill within a mere eighty years of its supposed discovery. It is difficult to believe that such advanced topiary had developed without some previous foundation, and, given the evident universal human compulsion to decorate any plain surface, one might reasonably assume that others elsewhere had already set a precedent.

As well as borrowing from other cultures, the Romans transmitted their own to subject nations, and the art of topiary along with it. In 43AD they came to Britain and remained there precariously for 400 years. During that time colonists settled and built themselves villas in imitation of those they had left behind in Italy. Although this was a short-lived attempt at civilized refinement and none of the villas survived for long after the Roman withdrawal from Britain, archaeologists have unearthed clear evidence for the existence of villa gardens that resemble those described by classical authors.

The most remarkable of these is at Fishbourne in Sussex, the site of a virtual palace built on a lavish scale by a Roman of presumably great wealth. The buildings were arranged around a large rectangular garden bisected by a wide walk and enclosed by other smaller paths. Along the sides of each of these have been found narrow trenches of rich soil, almost certainly dug out to provide cultivated beds for ornamental hedges which, on the evidence of Roman descriptions, would have been made of clipped box, much in the style popular in later centuries for edging kitchen garden beds. Of the plants themselves, nothing remains. More specific archaeological evidence has been found at Frocester in Gloucestershire, where excavation of a fourth-century villa garden has also revealed trenches dug for

In the restored garden of the House of the Vettii in Pompeii, clipped box bushes have been replaced exactly where the roots of the original plants remained after the eruption of Vesuvius in AD79.

hedges beside the paths, together this time with charcoal positively identified as having come from box plants. In Oxfordshire, too, charred debris from boxwood has been discovered during the exploration of a villa site.

The two species the Romans usually used for topiary were box and cypress. It seems likely that the latter was already indigenous to Britain, flourishing in the warmer conditions which prevailed at that time (Tacitus describes the British climate during the Roman occupation as 'awful, with frequent rain and fog, but no extreme cold'). As late as the seventeenth century Mediterranean cypresses were popular decorative trees in English gardens, although they have always been susceptible to sudden severe weather: in 1686 John Ray recorded in his *Historia plantarum* that savage frosts three years earlier killed nearly all the cypresses in the country. Today they grow in only the very mildest areas of Britain, and are not the valuable medium for topiary that they remain in warmer climates.

Box, however, is still a popular hedge and topiary plant. There is a strong possibility that it was introduced into England — and perhaps into other parts of the Empire — by the Romans, despite the fact that the plant has long been accepted as a 'native' species, for it does not show the even distribution across Europe that would be characteristic of a natural spread westwards. The earliest signs of its presence in Britain are associated with Roman settlements, particularly burial sites where it apparently had some ritual significance. Roman colonists are known to have imported grapes, cherries and walnuts for cultivation in villa gardens; with their enthusiasm for box topiary, they might be expected also to bring with them the species that played such a part in gardens back home.

Right across Europe, however, these elegant gardens were to disappear as the Roman Empire disintegrated. The centuries that followed, the so-called Dark Ages, were a time of social chaos and instability, hostile to the development of ornamental gardening which is primarily a luxury of settled and relatively wealthy cultures. On the fringe of the continent, in Byzantium, gardening lived on; Byzantine gardens are thought to have followed the Roman model and, on the evidence of clipped trees and arbours seen in mosaics, probably included topiary. Elsewhere, it seems that only in the comparative peace of monasteries or the medicinal herb gardens of fortified houses could anything other than essential crops be grown.

ITALY

From the fall of Rome in the fifth century until the early Renaissance in the twelfth and thirteenth centuries, the continuity of devotional life in monasteries, especially those of enclosed orders, gave many aspects of civilized life sanctuary from the political and social barbarism outside. The Carthusians, for example, were a totally enclosed order of monks, each following a solitary life of prayer and contemplation in a private cell. These cells were arranged around a cloistered courtyard of small individual gardens, such as those at the monastery in Va di Ema, Florence or that of the Certosa di Pavia, where low clipped hedges divide the cloister garden into small units. The Benedictines followed a rule of self-sufficiency and cultivated gardens for herbs, fruit and vegetables. Their cloisters, too,

were arranged around formal decorative gardens, designed both as an aid to meditation and to ensure a supply of flowers and foliage for the altar. It was in these surroundings that simple topiary seems to have survived.

Beyond the monastery wall in Italy political differences began to be resolved as smaller regions were consolidated into kingdoms, and during the thirteenth century the construction of gardens slowly revived in the new climate of comparative peace and wealth. A book on garden practice and theory, written by Petrus de Crescentiis at the turn of the fourteenth century, already clearly distinguishes between the gardens of ordinary people and those designed on a

Standard trees and a trained pergola in the background of this painting by Lorenzo Lotto (c. 1480–1556) record the contemporary Italian fashion for topiary.

grander scale for the nobility. For the latter he recommends planting tall narrow hedges for shelter, and clipping trees or training them on frameworks to form tunnels and arbours, even 'rooms and towers', remarking in passing that 'the rich... have the means to satisfy their desires, and need nothing except the knowledge and skill to carry out their plans'.

This time the knowledge and inspiration came not from foreign slaves or gardens, but from literature surviving from classical Rome and once more appreciated as part of the revival of interest in Italy's own past. The poet Petrarch looked to Virgil for guidance when designing a garden, while Leone Alberti, a highly educated man who included architecture amongst his many accomplishments, based his ideas about gardens on those of Pliny. Whole sections of Alberti's book on design, *De re aedificatoria*, published in 1452, echo both the spirit and the expressions of Pliny's letters.

The ancient Romans were found to be masters of many garden skills, and Alberti's reappraisal of these was reflected in the garden built in 1459 to his design at the Villa Quaracchi in Florence. This garden appears to have included classical features of all kinds, such as a grove and pergola, hedged orchards, walks bordered by clipped box, and above all topiary: 'spheres, porticoes, temples, vases, urns, apes, donkeys, oxen, a bear, giants, men and women, warriors, a witch, philosophers, Popes and cardinals'. The whole repertoire of Roman subjects seems once more to have become fashionable.

Alberti was not alone in his fascination with topiary. In 1467 a monk called Francesco Colonna, under the pseudonym of Polyphilius, published a long, illustrated allegorical story, *Hypnerotomachia*, recounting a vision many scenes of which were enacted in imaginary gardens. He encloses one garden with trees, perhaps trained as pleached screens according to his description of the 'strange twisting of the branches and their green leaves, so artfully intertwined and grown together'. Elsewhere he has clipped hedges of myrtle and cypress, and shaped junipers in large pots. Hyssop is trimmed into spheres, box into the shape of peacocks; one garden contained topiary of 'spun glass', another an enormous maze.

This maze would not fit the modern picture, inspired by the few famous examples in much later gardens, of an area divided by insuperable clipped hedges where the wanderer is challenged not to get lost; these have always been the exception. To the medieval or Renaissance mind, mazes were either labyrinths for penitential exercises painted on the floors of churches, or garden diversions cut in turf or often made with dwarf hedges of thyme, hyssop, box or lavender, seldom taller than knee-high. Colonna's dream version was a water labyrinth, designed to be sailed around and probably divided by similar low structures.

The extravagant dream catalogue also includes accounts and illustrations of elaborate parterres, whose hedges were made from trimmed artemisia, cotton lavender, germander, marjoram, thyme and rue. Despite its French name, the parterre is not exclusively part of the gardening tradition of France. Already by the middle of the fourteenth century gardens of Florentine houses included areas of ornamental beds arranged in patterns, an idea which might be traced back to the Roman custom of edging beds with low box hedges. These early Italian parterres do not seem to have yet developed the balanced patterns typical of the formal gardens of seventeenth-century France, patterns which could be fully appreciated only when viewed from above.

The *Hypnerotomachia* proved to be an enduring influence on subsequent Italian garden design, and Colonna's ideas were disseminated

Topiary designs taken from the Hypnerotomachia *range from the simple to the fantastical: those below were all designed in box or bay.*

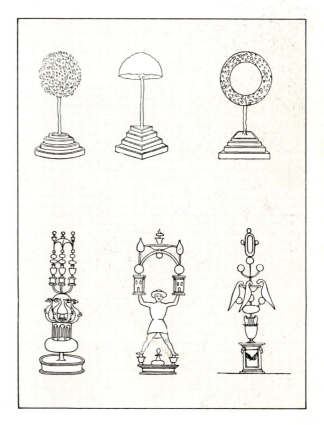

further by the borrowings of other writers such as Rabelais and Shakespeare. Most of the more practical garden features he described began to appear in a succession of notable grand gardens in many parts of Italy. In the sixteenth-century garden of the Villa Imperiale at Pesaro on the Adriatic coast, for example, grottoes, terraces, porticoes and pergolas abound. There is plenty of topiary, with citrus fruit trained as espaliers on the walls, parterres with clipped hedges of myrtle, rosemary or box, and pleached alleys of tall bay trees.

Pleaching seems to have become as popular as simple clipping for making dense ornamental hedges. When the French writer Montaigne visited the Medici garden at Castello, he was impressed by the number of pleached alleys 'thickly interwoven and covered with all sorts of

Though the more elaborate topiary of the typically Renaissance gardens of the Villa Imperiale has been lost, box parterres and citrus espaliers can be seen there today.

aromatic trees, such as cedars, cypresses, orange, lemon and olive trees, their branches mingled and intertwined so much that one can easily appreciate how the strongest sun cannot penetrate them. The trunks of the cypresses and other trees are planted in rows so close together that only three or four people might walk side by side.' He noticed, too, that above the gateways were suspended coats of arms 'made from the branches of trees, their natural growth encouraged and trained by various fastenings, and by pruning and tying'.

Despite the widespread occurrence of topiary in all its forms in Renaissance Italian gardens, it seems usually to have existed only as a structural element or decorative accent within a geometrical overall plan. Very rarely was a garden devoted entirely to a collection of topiary. At Castello Balduino, however, a medieval castle at Montalto di Pavia on the high slopes of the Appenines, a beautiful topiary garden of remarkable symmetry has survived the centuries.

The bold design of the Renaissance topiary garden at Castello Balduino depends entirely for its effect on simply carved blocks of yew.

The precise date of its creation is unknown. The bulky evergreens that fill the garden are clipped into simple abstract shapes and arranged in a pattern as satisfying to the modern as to the Renaissance eye.

The geometric severity of the topiary at Castello Balduino is contrasted by the fluid lines of the clipped yew hedges of another surviving Italian topiary garden, at the Villa Garzoni near Collodi in Tuscany (see illustration p.45). This garden was constructed in the middle of the seventeenth century and seems to show the liberating influence of Baroque ideas. While the Renaissance garden reflected the rule of balance and harmony, at the Villa Garzoni a sense of mischief, an irrepressible flamboyance, seems to have guided the hand that first cut the swirling designs.

This imaginative fusion of traditionally formal hedge-clipping with the more sculptural techniques of figurative topiary was, however, not to be developed in the years that followed. Instead the use of topiary throughout Europe was to be increasingly dominated by the regal magnificence of the French garden.

VERSAILLES AND BEYOND

The story of topiary in France was emphatically one of the development of hedges, whether as the framework of extensive parterres or as borders for alleys and rides through forested parkland. Renaissance ideas about garden design spread to France at an early date, as a result of the regular contact between neighbouring states and particularly of the periodical incursions of French armies on to Italian soil. Following campaigns in Italy at the end of the fifteenth century and again thirty years later, French soldiers brought home a memory of Italian achievements in gardening and a desire to emulate what they had seen.

By 1520 terrace beds in the garden at the castle of Gaillon, near Rouen, had been formally edged with hedges probably of scented herbs or box. According to an engraving of the gardens published by the architect Jacques du Cerceau in 1576, these level beds had been arranged in a series of small square patterns or knots, each enclosed by dwarf hedging which was also used to construct two low mazes. This was literally to set the pattern for later parterres, which increasingly resembled intricate embroidery, so much so that by the turn of the seventeenth century the design of gardens and garments could almost be considered a single craft. About 1600, for example, Pierre Vallet wrote a book about the royal gardens in which he worked, although he explicitly described himself as Henri IV's official embroiderer.

A contemporary of Vallet's, Olivier de Serres, produced a treatise on agriculture giving full instructions for creating a parterre. He suggested such extravagant designs as 'letters, patterns, shapes, coats of arms, men and animals, buildings and boats', made and edged with sweet-scented herbs — lavender, rosemary, sage and thyme amongst others — or with short bushes of myrtle and box. The last, he noted, was preferable to any of the others because a parterre made with it would be certain to last longer: 'the beauty of box foliage stays the same in any weather, even in ice and snow. Its hardiness gives it long life and easy maintenance.'

Claude Mollet, head gardener to the king, took de Serres' ideas further when explaining his own comprehensive principles for designing and siting parterres, especially the highly ornate *parterres de broderie*, within the overall scheme of a formal garden. Hitherto Italian influence had been clearly discernible in French gardens, perhaps most typically in that developed by Henri IV at the castle of St Germain-en-Laye on the bank of the Seine near Paris. (This has now disappeared, but contemporary accounts suggest it was a close reproduction of one of the great Renaissance villa gardens with simple parterres, clipped dividing hedges, and bushes trimmed into fantastic topiary figures.)

Mollet, however, established the mature concept of the formal garden, to be viewed from the house rather than explored as Italian gardens seemed to invite one to do. Wit, charm and inventiveness surrendered to discipline, to an imposition of logic and mathematical order on nature as far as could be seen from the upper windows of the house. André Le Nôtre, who stamped his own authority on countless gardens and who was reported to have said that he could not stand any restriction on a view, set about creating formal vistas that seemed to stretch to infinity through the countryside, first around the château at Vaux-le-Vicomte and later for Louis XIV at Versailles, where he began work in 1662.

The grandiose scale of this royal undertaking was remarkable. Preliminary civil engineering work — levelling ground, cutting roads and laying on water for the lakes and fountains — employed more than 30,000 men. And once the grounds were laid out and established, an army of gardeners would have been required simply to clip the high hedges of hornbeam which enclosed the woodland beyond the formal gardens. Trimming hedges on such a scale was a massive and continuous undertaking — a practical consideration seldom remembered by admiring visitors to estates designed in the expansive Versailles style. (Even today, with the benefit of modern power tools, clipping the relatively few miles of hedge at Chatsworth House in Derbyshire fully occupies three men from July to October.)

From Mollet's The Garden of Pleasure *(1670), this design is for a parterre 'partly embroidery, and partly knots of grass and flowers'.*

The restored gardens of Vaux-le-Vicomte still reflect the grandeur of Le Nôtre's original conception.

The great hedges at Versailles had a passive, architectural function, used to screen the natural woodland that lay beyond them and contain the area within in the same way as dwarf hedges around parterres. They can no longer be seen today: later remodelling, in particular extensive planting in the eighteenth century, has softened the lines of Le Nôtre's original plan. However, contemporary prints of Versailles and of Marly, a later project by Louis XIV and Le Nôtre, show great areas of trees organized into geometrical blocks by tall narrow hedges that run dead straight for their full length; nature there seems totally subjugated.

These are only illustrations, their mathematical precision no doubt exaggerated, although in an ideal world of French formalism the hedges would most certainly have grown in that way. They clearly demonstrate however the intentions of the design, by which plants were to be organised with a rigid authority symbolic of the power of the monarchy itself. The same absolutism was apparent in the training of topiary, which at Marly seems to have been confined to pleaching and shaping trees into architectural structures such as porticoes and colonnades: supreme examples of the topiarist's skill but somehow denying any life to the trees used.

No wonder William Robinson, the British nineteenth-century iconoclast and supporter of a less restrained style of gardening, referred to 'the deadly formalism of Versailles'. Reaction was inevitable, but it was a long time gathering strength. In the meantime the ideas of Mollet and Le Nôtre spread across Europe, influencing the development of gardens until well into the eighteenth century, even as far away as Russia where Peter the Great returned from his European travels to create an outstanding garden in the French style at Peterhof, Leningrad. It is the only garden of its kind in the Soviet Union, although elements of the formal style were adopted elsewhere, as in the Nikitsky Garden at Yalta where avenues are bordered by walls of clipped evergreen oak or low box hedges.

In Denmark the gardens at Hirschholm and the castle of Fredericksborg were based on the style of Versailles, while Queen Christina imported Andre Mollet, Claude's son, to Sweden to design the layout of the royal estate at Jakobsdal. Le Nôtre himself advised on the construction of the palace gardens at Drottningholm, near Stockholm, where the hedged walks and parterres started a fashion for embroidered beds and box topiary that can still be seen at Sturefors Castle and at Sandemar.

In Germany, too, the grand French manner supplanted the style of the Italian Renaissance garden. The change is evident from the early seventeenth century; while several private gardens are recorded as laid out in characteristic Renaissance style with box parterres, pleached enclosures and potted topiary, the gardens planned for the castle at Heidelberg were to consist of enormous terraces cut into the steep hillside and patterned with elaborate square parterres.

The most notable survivor of the formal gardens of this period in Germany is that at Brühl, created for Augustus, Archbishop of Cologne, by the French designer Girard in the early eighteenth century. Although the layout was later

The formal deciduous hedges at Schönbrunn, shown here in a print c. 1800, survive to this day; in the past they were clipped from mobile wooden scaffolds.

considerably altered, twentieth-century restoration using the original plans has re-created the elaborate swirling parterre, low clipped edging and the square-cut stilt hedges characteristic of the French approach. In Hungary and Austria, too, gardens followed the same irresistible path; in the park and botanic garden at Schönbrunn, Vienna, for example, enormous clipped hedges and shrubs trimmed to abstract shapes are immediately recognizable as having been inspired by Le Nôtrean ideals.

Even China did not remain entirely immune to Versailles. Just outside Peking, at Yuan Ming Yuan or the 'Garden of Bright Perfection', a succession of emperors from 1730 onwards created and elaborated a vast complex of cultivated mountains and lakes. These were recorded both in a series of paintings and, for Europeans, in letters from Jesuit missionaries. In 1740 the Jesuits themselves were commissioned to build for the Emperior Qian Long a set of 'European palaces' in the style of Versailles, whose grounds included pavilions, a maze or parterre and a

In the eighteenth-century park of the Château of Beloeil in Belgium, fine hornbeam hedges are set amongst mature unclipped trees.

great fountain: in fact a complete miniature garden in the grand formal manner was established as a curiosity of European artifice in the midst of that lavish, equally artificial, Chinese landscape. Fortunately that was as far as western ideas were allowed to go; the gardens later decayed and Chinese garden tradition continued unaffected.

In Europe, other styles of gardening also persisted alongside the French. Italy largely went its own way, though Le Nôtre himself was commissioned to design the great formal plans for the Quirinal and Vatican gardens in Rome. Two other areas with strong gardening traditions — Spain and the Netherlands — adopted as many ideas from the Italians as the French, and instead of embracing the foreign styles unreservedly, imparted to them a regional character. In Spain, for example, Moorish influence remained alive despite the imported veneer of Italian Renaissance elements such as designs in box and geometrical beds — the latter prominent in the public parks at El Retiro and the Jardín de la Isla, both in Madrid. The grand manner did not destroy the intimacy of the Moorish gardens of

Andalusia, with their cool courtyards and burbling water courses: even box parterres and crenellated cypress hedges shed their formal severity around the pools of the Generalife.

In neighbouring Portugal, Italy rather than France was again the more dominant influence, and the gardens at Bemfica with simple dense parterres and clipped shrubs are typical of the more compact Italian style. Dutch gardens likewise tended to be small, something of a limitation when compared with the sprawling grandeur of Versailles. But the Dutch were already accustomed to using confined spaces to best effect, filling their gardens with small formal ornaments and decorative beds. The predominantly level ground was ideal both for water and simple parterres, features that could be adapted and scaled down from the French model.

Topiary lent itself equally well to use in confined places. French designers had tended to use clipped trees merely as elements in a geometrical composition, but the Dutch appreciated the more individual qualities of specimen topiary. Of all the varied ingredients of the Renaissance and Versailles styles, it was figurative topiary that was most widely adopted in Dutch gardens, with interesting later consequences for its development in Britain.

BRITAIN

Britain, too, felt the influence of Versailles. In the late seventeenth century, while Le Nôtre made plans for London's Greenwich Park, laid out in long straight avenues stretching up the hill, great gardens throughout the country imitated his style with parterres, tall hedges and expanses of disciplined woodland. However, as in the Netherlands, local taste and tradition were to lead to different interpretations of his ideas and to a long-standing, quite un-French, fascination with the more eccentric forms of topiary.

John Loudon, the nineteenth-century garden journalist, speculated that after the Norman Conquest in the eleventh century the lost Roman style of gardening may have been reintroduced into Britain. There is in fact little contemporary reference to ornamental gardening apart from vague literary allusions, most of which are suspiciously allegorical. Nevertheless, the period of growing prosperity which followed the arrival of the Normans doubtless saw the establishment of many undocumented pleasure gardens by the nobility, and as elsewhere in Europe by the twelfth century a craze was developing for mazes and labyrinths.

Improved methods of agriculture and gardening were certainly brought from the continent, including novel plants and varieties. It is interesting to note that these probably included gooseberries and other soft fruit, which were often to be used for decorative purposes, even as fruit hedges. The first definite record of gooseberries in Britain occurs in 1275 when Edward I was supplied with bushes imported from France for the royal gardens. These were probably used in the same way as they were on the continent; in the mid-sixteenth century the German writer on husbandry, Heresbachius, recorded that a fruit he called ribes 'with red and rich berries [was] a common bush used for enclosing of gardens and making of borders and herb gardens. It will easily grow but that it is something troublesome, by reason of its sharp prickles, to be bent about summer houses.' (Whether the account is referring to gooseberries or redcurrants is not quite clear.)

It is in fact only from the sixteenth century onwards that a reliable picture of British gardening, and of the role topiary played in it, begins to emerge. In 1502 the Duke of Buckingham is recorded as having made special payments to his gardeners for 'diligence in making knots and for clipping of knots' — early evidence of bonuses for skilled work. Henry VII, we know, created 'fair and pleasant' gardens at Richmond Palace, filled

The popularity of knot gardens was such that many designs were published. This one is taken from T. Hyll's The Profitable Art of Gardening *(1568).*

with knot gardens and parterres embellished with designs of 'many marvellous beasts as lions, dragons and others of diverse kind'.

These gardens, however, were eclipsed by the magnificent developments set in motion in the 1520s at Hampton Court by his successor, Henry VIII, with the help of professional Italian gardeners. Included there was a great variety of topiary, according to the Oxford botanist, Dr Robert Plot, who wrote in 1677 that the garden had been 'long celebrated for its trees cut into grotesque forms, which Dr Plot admired and dignified with the name of Topiary Works' — recording his own use of a translation of the Latin *topiarii operis*, perhaps the first appearance of the English term. Hampton Court was not the only such undertaking; Henry VIII's antiquary, John Leland, wrote with approval of the orchard at Wressel Castle in Yorkshire where there were 'mounts, *opere topiario*, written about with degrees like the turnings in cockle shells', and of a garden at Little Haseley near Oxford with 'marvellous fair walks, *topiarii operis*, and orchards and pools'. Topiary is still an outstanding feature of the gardens at Haseley Court.

With the king setting the pace, many gardens besides these quickly followed: the topiary garden of clipped yews at Heslington near York and the huge 'elephant' hedge of yew at Rockingham Castle, Northamptonshire, both date from about 1560 according to the historian Lady Amherst. By 1618 William Lawson in his *A New Orchard and*

Garden described to country housewives how they should organize their gardens. Although fruit trees and shrubs were of greatest importance, 'your gardener can frame your lesser wood to the shape of men armed in the field, ready to give battle; of swift-running grey hounds, or of well-scented and true-running hounds to chase the deer or hunt the hare'. Among plants recommended for edging and clipping Lawson includes rosemary; forty years previously, Barnaby Googe had noted that women commonly trimmed rosemary into various shapes 'as in the fashion of a cart, a peacock, or such things as they fancy'. Not that hedges were merely passive ornament, though, for housewives of the time used them 'for the drying of linen, cloths and yarns'.

For anyone intending to cultivate topiary in the early seventeenth century, the great gardening writer and botanist to Charles II, John Parkinson, had valuable practical advice to offer; it is still valid today. While accepting the versatility of yew, he tried to encourage the more imaginative use of privet, because 'to make hedges or arbours in gardens it is so apt that no other can be like unto it, to be cut, lead and drawn into what form one will, either of beasts, birds or men armed or otherwise'.

The roots of box hedging were, he conceded, invasive and liable to rob the soil nearby of nutrients. The remedy was simple, yet it was:

... a secret known but unto few, which is this: you shall take a broad pointed iron like unto a slice or chisel, which thrust down right into the ground a good depth all along the inside of the border of box somewhat close thereunto, you may thereby cut away the spreading roots thereof, which draw so much moisture from the other herbs on the inside, and by this means both preserve your herbs and flowers in the knot, and your box also for that the box will be nourished sufficiently from the rest of the roots it shooteth on all the other sides.

A spade is the best modern version of a broad pointed iron, but the principle is the same.

Topiary did not however receive unanimous support from gardeners then any more than now, and even as Parkinson was working on his book *Paradisi in sole paradisus terrestris* in 1625, Francis Bacon published his learned essay *Of Gardens*. Although nearly a hundred years were to elapse before reaction to over-ornate formal gardening gathered strength, Bacon was dissenting already from the generally universal enthusiasm for

The sombre group of yew topiary at Packwood House,
The Sermon on the Mount, dates from the mid-seventeenth
century.

A bird's-eye view of an estate at Llanerch in Denbighshire, 1662, shows the formal use of trees in the seventeenth-century British garden.

topiary. He would have nothing to do with prettily patterned knot gardens to be enjoyed from upper windows or from viewing mounts; 'they be but toys: you may see as good sights, many times, in tarts.' Nor was he very keen on specimen topiary. 'For the ordering of the ground within the great hedge, I leave it to variety of device, advising nevertheless that whatsoever form you cast it into, first it be not too busy or full of work. Wherein I, for my part, do not like images cut out in juniper or other garden stuff: they be for children.' Yet his was not a blanket condemnation: he conceded that other equally ornate decoration would appear in his ideal garden.

For many years his criticism of topiary seems to have stood alone. In 1632 the main entrance of Oxford Botanic Garden, then known as the Physic Garden, was flanked by a pair of enormous topiary giants. About twenty years later at Packwood House, Warwickshire, the famous topiary garden of clipped yews was established, popularly known as The Sermon on the Mount, although it takes a little imagination to appreciate this description, apparently based on nothing more than one

gardener's explanation. Public approval for topiary was endorsed by John Evelyn in his enthusiastic study, *Sylva.* If anyone appreciated trees grown for their own beauty and use, he did, but he was not above adapting them too for garden ornament. On the subject of yew, for example, he advised his readers to transplant seedlings at three years old:

> Form them into standards, knobs, walks, hedges, etc, in all which works they succeed marvellous well and are worth our patience for their perennial verdure and durableness. I do again name them for hedges, preferably for beauty, and a stiff defence to any plant I have ever seen, and may upon that account (without vanity) be said to be the first which brought it into fashion, as well for defence as a *succedaneum* for cypress, whether in hedges, or pyramids, conic-spires, bowls, or what other shapes, adorning the parks or other avenues with their lofty tops thirty foot high, and braving all the efforts of the most rigid winter which cypress cannot weather.

Twenty-five years later, in 1689, William of Orange came to the English throne, bringing with him from the Netherlands a typically

Dutch passion for elaborately clipped evergreens. It is sometimes maintained that the national enthusiasm for topiary originated with his arrival, on the grounds of Daniel Defoe's comments: '[William] was particularly delighted with the decoration of evergreens as the greatest addition to the beauty of a garden. With this particular judgement all the gentlemen of England began to fall in, and in a few years fair gardens and fine houses began to grow up in every corner.' As far as topiary is concerned, however, we have seen how much interest already existed, and it probably needed only slight royal approval as a catalyst to explode into near obsession. Sir William Temple seems to have laid out his Dutch garden at Moor Park some time before the King's accession; a mere three years after it, Levens Hall with its world-famous garden of intricate and bizarre topiary was started.

Not long after William's accession, evidence of the popularity of topiary appears in the comments Celia Fiennes makes throughout her record of a journey *Through England on a Side*

Espaliered trees, topiary and an ornate parterre all feature in this idealized eighteenth-century garden from Laurence's The Clergyman's Recreation *(1714).*

Saddle in the time of William and Mary, published in 1694. Her constant and admiring references to clipped trees, cut topiary and stilt hedges with 'platted' branches wherever she went testifies to the general acceptance of this formal or, as it became known, 'Dutch' style. In fact she roundly disapproves of the gardens at Haddon Hall because they had 'nothing very curious as the mode now is'. Topiary had, as she said, become a fad and therein lay the threat of reaction, for fashion is always transient. Several years were to elapse, however, before the inevitable purge of garden topiary, which was to be indulged to as great excess as the craze it succeeded.

While Dutch William did not actually introduce topiary to Britain his accession certainly extended the reign of the shears. Hitherto suitable evergreens, either as developed topiary or plants ready for training, had often been imported from Dutch nurseries, renowned for their proficiency in the art. With the enormous growing demand for these shrubs there was an obvious opening for anyone enterprising enough to start a specialist nursery, and that man was George London. He already had a flourishing 100-acre nursery established in 1681 at Brompton Road, London, on a site now occupied by museums. Eight years later he was joined by Henry Wise, and on his own appointment as Deputy Superintendent of the Royal Gardens, it was inevitable that the firm should start to specialize in the king's favoured style of garden design.

This is not the only claim to fame of London and Wise — it is often forgotten that their nursery introduced countless new plants to English gardens — but their popular reputation (to the next generation, notoriety) rested on their expertise in the Dutch school of gardening. In later years when this style was proscribed, the essayist William Hazlitt described the company's speciality as 'that preposterous plan of deforming Nature by making her statuesque, and reducing her irregular and luxuriant lines to a dead and prosaic level through the medium of the shears. Gods, animals, and other objects were no longer carved out of stone; but the trees, shrubs and hedges were made to do double service as a body of verdure and a sculpture gallery.'

While even today royal opinion can start a sudden fashion, writers no longer hold their former command of the world of ideas, and it is difficult now to appreciate that in the eighteenth century an essay or article by a prominent figure could start a revolution amongst its wealthy and educated readers. With King William gone, leaving British gardens uniformly crammed with a clipped extravagance of 'giants, animals, monsters, coats of arms and mottoes in yew, box and holly', as Horace Walpole wrote with hindsight, it needed little to turn modish opinion against fanciful topiary. In 1711 the Third Earl of Shaftesbury wrote 'I shall no longer resist the passion for things of a natural kind: where neither Art, nor the Conceit or Caprice of Man has spoiled their genuine order by breaking in upon the Primitive State.'

The following year Addison launched his attack in *The Spectator*.

> Our British Gardeners ... instead of honouring Nature, love to deviate from it as much as possible. Our trees rise in Cones, Globes and Pyramids. We see the Marks of the Scissors upon every Plant and Bush. For my own part, I would rather look upon a Tree in all its Luxuriancy and Diffusion of Boughs and Branches, than when it is thus cut and Trimmed into a Mathematical Figure.

Pope supported the rebellion with his typically satirical catalogue of topiary, from 'St George in box; his arm scarce long enough, but will be in condition to stick the dragon by next April' to 'a quickset [hawthorn] hog, shot up into a porcupine by its being forgot one week in rainy weather'.

The reaction was as extreme as the establishment against which it rebelled. No-one could see at that stage that the new landscape style was as

Repton's design for Aspley Cottage at Woburn, from his Red Book *of 1804, includes specimen topiary, a maze and a trained arcade in the picturesque lodge garden.*

artificial as clipping trees into whimsical sculpture. The movement gathered momentum, first with Charles Bridgeman, who succeeded Wise in charge of the royal gardens, and then William Kent, a landscape designer who according to one contemporary report 'imitated nature even in all her blemishes, and planted dead trees and mole-hills in opposition to parterres and quincunxes'. Lancelot ('Capability') Brown worked for both men in turn before starting as a designer in his own right; under his influence, what had begun with a few individuals straining after a sublime and somewhat sentimental natural innocence, was transformed into a destructive surge of popular opinion.

Gardens everywhere were destroyed in the name of pictorial landscape, their carefully nurtured formal ornaments scrapped as hills were raised and trees left untrimmed to form contrived Romantic views. Robert Southey, visiting New College in Oxford in 1807, noted that the new landscape and later the picturesque styles offered nothing in replacement.

> The College arms were formerly cut in box, and the alphabet grew around them; in another compartment was a sun-dial in box, set round with true lovers' knots. These have been destroyed more easily as well as more rapidly than they were formed; but, as nothing beautiful has been substituted in their places, it had been better if they had suffered these old oddities to have remained.

The 'Mon Plaisir' garden in the grounds of Elvaston Castle in Derbyshire, designed between 1830 and 1850, made extravagant use of topiary. (Picture from E. A. Brooke's The Gardens of England.*)*

By the time he was writing fashion was turning again. Disenchantment with the vogue for 'un-groomed' countryside was widespread but it was too late for countless examples of topiary, erased by Kent, Brown and their numerous disciples in their crusade against tradition. In 1772 Sir William Chambers had warned that 'unless the mania were not checked, in a few years longer there would not be found three trees in a line from Land's End to the Tweed'. Happily, a few examples were left and survive to this day in notable formal gardens, but it was to take time before popular disillusion with the landscape movement led to a revival of more classical garden craft.

In 1803 Humphry Repton challenged the whole philosophy of the movement: 'Why this art has been called 'landscape-gardening' perhaps he who gave it the title may explain. I can see no reason, unless it be the efficacy which it has shown in destroying landscapes, in which, indeed, it seems infallible.' In the middle of the nineteenth century Sir Charles Barry and W. A. Nesfield were starting to recreate formal gardens whose design included parterres and other Renaissance elements, although these tended to seem more a return to orthodoxy than a development of style.

The first visible signs of a revival of topiary other than as an architectural feature in period gardens appeared at the end of the nineteenth century on the Rothschild estate at Ascott, Buckinghamshire, where a winter garden was created of golden yews shaped as 'animals and birds of almost every kind, with tables, chairs, churches, and other objects', including a magnificent topiary sundial. Two firms of nurserymen, William Cutbush & Son in London and Cheal & Sons in Sussex, encouraged the reawakened interest by specializing in the production of topiary 'off the shelf', and several contemporary photographs show their standing grounds or exhibition displays packed with birds, spirals, boats and tables shaped from yew and box.

A century earlier, Walpole had tried to discourage gardeners from creating formal decoration in a garden on the grounds of the skill he said it required: 'I should hardly advise any of these attempts in the form of gardens amongst us; they are adventures of too hard achievement for any common hands.' Despite this tribute, unintended no doubt, to the craftsmen gardeners of the past, Victorian self-confidence proved with its exuberance for all things horticultural that the techniques could be revived.

NORTH AMERICA

After the acrimonious debate that raged in British gardens like a horticultural civil war, it is a relief to turn to the far less volatile story of topiary in America. Transatlantic remoteness and the variety offered by the wide range of garden habitats across a large continent have provided relative freedom from the dogmatic movements that continually transformed the European scene, while encouraging the preservation of local examples of each major style.

The immediate demands of ensuring survival in a hostile country would have prevented early American settlers from indulging in such a luxury. Nevertheless, there is evidence from a map that in 1604 allowance was made in plans for developing Neutral Island in the St Croix river for small formal gardens, perhaps to be laid out as parterres. Whether these were actually made is uncertain, but it is unlikely that the gardening instincts of the first settlers remained dormant for long.

By the time a century had passed there was sufficient stability for the whole range of garden crafts to flourish, as excavations at Williamsburg, Virginia, have shown. During work on the Governor's Palace, restored to its original appearance as in the early eighteenth century, all kinds of tools and equipment were unearthed. The evidence of these together with numerous

An Italian Renaissance garden with topiary and parterres was recreated early this century at the Villa Vizcaya in subtropical Florida.

contemporary accounts has ensured the authenticity of the reconstruction, which includes over ninety acres of gardens containing amongst other typical features of the period parterres with clipped box edging, a maze in clipped holly, and formal specimen topiary in various architectural shapes such as cones and spirals. They give evidence that the European continental style was as enthusiastically embraced by American settlers as by gardeners in England.

Topiary has remained a feature of important American gardens ever since. Many of the gardens laid out in formal patterns for eighteenth century owners of large houses can still be seen in Virginia and Maryland. At Gunston Hall, Virginia, for example, there are rows of rectangular beds of flowers and specimen shrubs, each surrounded by substantial clipped box hedges, while at Mount Vernon, George Washington's Virginia home, a parterre of ornate beds edged with box reflects the continuing influence of French designs long after English gardeners had turned to landscape.

The landscape style did belatedly affect American design, although not with such profound impact. Whereas in England formal gardens were destroyed to make way for the landscapers, across the Atlantic it was new gardens or parks that tended to incorporate these ideas, encouraged by the writings of Andrew Downing in the mid-nineteenth century. Nevertheless, gardens continued to be made in the formal style, either wholly or in part, well into the twentieth century, some of them deliberate recreations such as the Renaissance-style garden of scrolled parterres and clipped evergreens at the Villa Vizcaya in Miami.

By far the most extraordinary collection of figurative topiary, in the tradition of the more fanciful Italian and before them Roman villa gardens, was created between 1905 and 1940 at the small country estate of Thomas Brayton in Portsmouth, Rhode Island. Within the semi-formal gardens his gardener, Joseph Carriero, developed a unique menagerie of clipped trees, some in classic geometrical forms, but most of them large representations of animals and birds: a giraffe, elephant, lion, camel, unicorn, two peacocks and a reindeer amongst many others. The gardens, aptly named Green Animals, continue to be developed and maintained today.

At Monkton, Maryland, the Ladew Topiary Gardens were developed virtually single-handed by Harvey S. Ladew during the first half of this century, a diverse collection of clipped decorated hedges and intricate evergreen sculpture.

Another striking collection of topiary has been created in the botanical gardens at Longwood near Kennet Square, Pennsylvania, where several smaller specialist gardens have been designed in one or more of the European traditions.

The range of climates across the USA has made it necessary to use plants other than those customary in Europe: at Villa Vizcaya, for example, parterres are edged with evergreen shrubby jasmine (*J. simplicifolium*) instead of box. At Longwood, hemlock and arbor-vitae (thuja), rather than the less hardy cypress, give vertical accents; even the dwarf box 'Suffruticosa' has not proved totally reliable in the harsh Pennsylvania winters.

Yet while the materials and techniques of European topiary have required modification, the styles have transplanted directly. Indeed, it is the ease with which foreign traditions have been assimilated, with perhaps several co-existing on the same site, that distinguishes American gardens from European counterparts which usually belong more recognizably to a particular movement or era. Only in the last hundred years have coherent styles developed in American garden design, notably those of the Country Place movement of Frederick Olmsted and his

At the Walter Hunnewell Arboretum in Wellesley, Massachusetts, European and oriental styles are blended.

followers, a formal approach for large estates that was made obsolete in the 1930s by the Great Depression, and the California School inspired by the architect Thomas Church.

When Church wrote his visionary book *Gardens Are For People* (1955) he established the principles by which, whether consciously or otherwise, many modern gardens are designed. Although historical authenticity still motivates a few studious recreations, most designers feel at liberty to use features and styles typical of several different nations or periods, blending them in an harmonious layout that is tailored to the site and the owner's requirements. Church himself first studied Californian gardens made by Spanish settlers who had imported the characteristic Moorish concept of enclosed courtyard gardens, and used them to form outdoor living areas that were an extension of the house itself. Within these, elements from a multiplicity of foreign styles could be incorporated.

American garden design was also influenced by the gardens of Japan, where the traditional ideal garden represented a 'borrowed landscape', with all its natural features reproduced in miniature. Evergreen shrubs and trees often required careful pruning to size in the *bonseki* style, a kind of landscape topiary only distantly related to the European tradition of clipping plants into simple architectural accents, since Japanese gardeners aim for softer, more natural outlines than those typical of classical topiary. One feature common to both traditions is the use of clipped hedges and screens in which branches are sometimes trained into place by 'stone-bending' — redirecting their growth by suspending stones from their tips.

One uniquely oriental method of training, which has been adopted by American topiarists, is 'cloud-pruning', in which the interesting stem structure of certain trees is artfully revealed by trimming the foliage into separate shaped masses; it is a style seen more often in Thailand and Hong Kong than in Japan where the result is considered too stiff and formal. In America, the technique has sometimes been successfully modified to produce a modern, almost Cubist effect of interlocking angular shapes. More fundamental however to the development of the modern style than the adaptation of technique is the assimilation of principles from the oriental tradition, and that of Japan in particular: the precise control of space and form even within a simple courtyard area, the careful integration of plants and architecture found in Church's work. The consequences for topiary could still be further developed.

THE CONTINUING TRADITION

When, in the late nineteenth century, the British topiary revival gathered pace, the nurseryman Herbert Cutbush toured Holland in search of topiary specimens for import into Britain. There he found the tradition still very much alive both amongst nurserymen, particularly in the Boskoop area, and in private gardens. Some of the best specimens he discovered in the gardens of remote Dutch farmhouses, and many of these he bought for re-sale from his nursery as the famous 'Cutbush's cut bushes'. The tradition of the craft had in fact never been eclipsed in Holland, and numerous examples can still be seen there today, both in domestic gardens and in those recreated or preserved on major sites, such as at Het Loo or the great formal gardens at the castle of Weldam.

It should have been no surprise to find so much interest surviving amongst ordinary gardeners in Holland; small private gardens in England (and Switzerland where formal box hedging never lost its popularity) have always shown the same kind of continuity and resistance to grand fashions. The history of gardens tends inevitably to concern itself mainly with famous or influential names in the same way that political history records Julius Caesar's crossing of the Rubicon but ignores the thousands who crossed with or after him. Yet many traditional plants and techniques, amongst them figurative topiary, owe their survival in large part to the conservatism of generations of cottage gardeners.

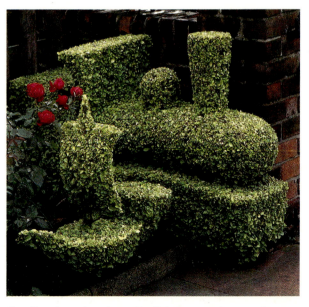

Small-scale topiary in an English front garden translates an age-old tradition into twentieth-century forms and an urban setting.

Box hedges outline vegetable beds in a modern farm garden in Switzerland.

Clipped trees and hedges probably first appeared in cottage gardens in imitation of specimens in grand gardens where some of the cottagers would have been employed. Just as the gardens of Roman nobility were maintained by skilled slaves, so the real work on the estates of those who later championed or derided particular styles was carried out by gardeners who as today would have known far more about the craft than their employers. With their privileged access to suitable plants and sound experience of the art, it was natural that employed gardeners should reproduce examples of topiary in their own gardens, and by the traditional cottage pattern of exchange and imitation the practice spread. Today some of the best examples of topiary can be seen in small rural gardens and in those of towns and suburbs where cottage-gardening techniques have been revived.

Classical topiary features are carefully maintained today in preserved gardens such as, in Britain, at Levens Hall in Cumbria or Packwood House in Warwickshire. Elsewhere, authentic reconstructions have been made, of which the imaginative French Renaissance gardens at Villandry are an outstanding example. Such conservation is essential, for too much has been destroyed in the past through social upheaval or merely ideological change.

These are fundamentally museum exhibits, however, reminding us of a heritage beyond which gardens, domestic ones especially, continue to evolve. Topiary is a live form of decorative or representational sculpture, and like its fine-art counterpart is a suitable medium for modern ideas. A steam locomotive carved from a hedge in an English front garden is as legitimate a design as any medieval coat of arms in box or turreted yew hedge. There is scope for experiment with topiary to accompany the increasingly catholic tastes evident in 'gardens for the people' everywhere, legitimate successors to the cottage garden, and only purists will condemn the emergence of a contemporary topiary idiom, even though it may at times seem to take the form of a fanciful fashion for box teddy bears.

DESIGN

Increasingly these days garden planning is becoming an unnecessarily sophisticated subject, clouded by the tendentious jargon of theorists who fancifully divide the garden into 'axes' and 'planes', and turn planning into an art form. Yet for most practical gardeners, the first priority is still the welfare of their plants. In the words of one head gardener of the old school, 'forget all this design taradiddle, and concentrate on making the plants happy. If you do this the rest of the garden will fall into place.'

It may not always seem quite so easy, but fortunately, concentrating on good husbandry will often suggest the most appropriate design scheme. Thus many of the most satisfying gardens have been created by ordinary gardeners unconcerned with design principles but very sensitive to the practical needs of their plants and the character of the garden in which they work. For commonsense, tempered with imagination and experience, is the basis of effective design.

For example, a hedge needs to go somewhere. This might seem obvious, yet very often hedges planted within gardens start or finish abruptly instead of leading naturally to a point of emphasis such as a specimen tree, gateway or boundary. A hedge should guide the eye somewhere special, preferably without your realizing consciously that it is directing you there. Topiary too will have a strong impact on the garden. Even a solitary specimen will draw attention and possibly reduce the prominence of neighbouring plants or features. Here, both aesthetics and the good of the plants themselves demand that overcrowding is avoided.

Before considering the details, the final forms and species, it is essential to consider the projected topiary or hedge in the entire context of the garden, not just as it is now but as it will be in ten, twenty, perhaps fifty years' time. While annuals are cleared in the autumn and herbaceous perennials can be moved about the garden, the plants discussed in this book have long lives and need to be left in one place to become established. Topiary and clipped hedges are generally formal in character, and therefore blend most easily into a fairly disciplined layout.

Serpentine beech hedges flank a quarter-mile walk at Chatsworth House in Derbyshire.

Mixing informal plantings with trimmed shrubs is not impossible — cottage gardeners have done this successfully for centuries — but requires a touch of inspiration or instinctive artlessness.

Once the overall intention is clear, then the imagination can play on all the possible styles and shapes, and on the different types of foliage, pictured in relation to the rest of the plants in the garden. Not only are the designs suitable for topiary unlimited, but a wide range of colours and textures are available in hedging plants, from the opulence of copper beech and the autumn tints of *Cotoneaster simonsii* to the soft greys of lavender or santolina and the bright red young growth of *Photinia* 'Red Robin'.

Consider also how the hedge will look in winter. When herbaceous plants in the garden have died down and many shrubs lost their leaves, an evergreen hedge will temporarily become a prominent feature, a deciduous one a less effective screen. Specimen topiary, nearly always trained from evergreen species, can suddenly look very isolated and conspicuous when surrounding plants have all died back, although a carefully placed clipped figure or group is valuable for retaining winter interest in an otherwise bare corner.

HEDGES

Planting a hedge as a boundary around a garden satisfies the natural instinct to enclose one's property, but also outlines its edges, turning the garden into a kind of outdoor room with a defined structure and character, depending on the type of hedge chosen. The strict lines of precisely clipped hedging, for example, impose a firm discipline that can be echoed within the garden by formal beds and neat plant arrangements. On the other hand, surrounding a rambling, informal garden with restrained clipped hedges can create an exciting contrast and clearly divide the world outside from the wilderness within.

The height of a boundary hedge will affect the character of the enclosed space, in addition to modifying growing conditions within. Tall hedges make a garden look smaller, not necessarily a disadvantage where seclusion or intimacy is intended. The apparent size of larger gardens is less dramatically altered by tall hedging, which may confer grandeur, especially if selectively placed openings allow glimpses of the view beyond. In these situations a lower hedge might appear ridiculously out of scale and fail to give a clear outline to the garden.

Hedges can vary in height according to species and situation from an edging of dwarf box no more than 15cm (6in) high to a tall screen of beech, one of the largest examples of which, at Meikleour in Perthshire, Scotland, has reached 30m (100ft) after almost 250 years. Width, too, varies widely, and should be considered in relation to the available room and intended effect. The narrowest practicable width is about 15cm (6in) for a dwarf hedge, 22cm (9in) for a slender screen of clipped beech or *Lonicera nitida*. On the other hand, the long stilt hedges of pleached limes on the South Lawn at Chatsworth are each 5.5m (18ft) wide, and many old billowing yew hedges are much wider still.

Hedging can be used within a large garden to divide it into two or more compartments, which may be planted in distinct styles or reserved for different activities. Even in a smaller garden the vegetable plot could be separated by a hedge of gooseberries or a narrow line of clipped beech to provide both shelter and division without actually excluding the productive area

from view. Deciding the height of such internal hedges depends on whether you prefer to see beyond one compartment to the next or intend an element of surprise as you pass from one to the other.

Shape, too, is modified by strategically placed hedging. For example, a long narrow garden will appear less so if a hedge is led midway from each side to conceal most of the far end, or from one side almost to the other, leaving an opening to frame a small part of the view beyond. The opposite effect can be achieved by running hedges lengthways down a squarer garden; here they will tend to increase its apparent length while reducing its width. More dramatically, a pair of hedges could be planted to form a corridor part of the way down the garden, exploiting its shape by guiding the visitor to a hidden room at the far end. A simple hedge of plants with golden rather than dark foliage at the foot of the garden will also make it look longer. It is all a matter of creating illusion within a given space.

Yew hedges provide the structure of the garden at Sissinghurst, Kent, dividing the area into compartments and at the same time making a dark foil for seasonal flowering plants.

ART CENTER COLLEGE OF DESIGN LIBRARY
1700 LIDA STREET
PASADENA, CALIFORNIA 91103

As can be seen, hedges lead or intervene as well as define, an important function where they are planted within the garden. When planning the design of a hedge, visualize first the views from given points and the way in which these would be interrupted or modified. Imagine, too, the experience of being guided by its intervention away from or towards more distant parts of the garden; and consider whether the diversion will be practical as well as aesthetically pleasing — for a hedge that looks right from the house can prove a nuisance if you often need to reach the garden beyond. Remember that an internal hedge must also look right from the other side when you turn round to face the way you have come. It need not, however, look the same; one side can be kept trimmed to provide a formal background, while the other is allowed to grow in a more relaxed style.

SPECIMEN TOPIARY

Shaped topiary is more static, and only rarely provides a garden with the kind of movement or structural definition that can be derived from carefully placed hedging. There are some notable exceptions, in particular the extraordinary fox hunt that seems to race across the lawn at the famous Ladew Topiary Gardens in Maryland, (see p.79), or another topiary pack of hounds at Knightshayes Court in Devon, running and

Slim hawthorn hedges enclose individual plots in a beautifully tended Danish allotment garden. The rounded faces of the hedges emphasize their winding course.

leaping along the tops of the clipped enclosure hedges (see p.68), bringing the otherwise formal garden dramatically to life. Generally, however, topiary has a function similar to that of statuary: it provides focal emphasis and, in the case of figurative pieces, populates otherwise impersonal surroundings.

Depending on the type of shape to be cut or trained, topiary can create an air of formality, even grandeur where elaborate specimens or groups are made. Yet, as many cottage gardens prove, designs which in isolation or a less intimate setting might seem formal and imposing can bring unique character and atmosphere to a garden. Simple geometrical designs can relieve the bareness of an area or give architectural form to a hedge or lawn; or a freestanding specimen in box or golden privet will brighten a dark corner which in turn will make an effective frame for the figure. Depending on the gardener's intention, topiary can be made to blend into its background, or on the other hand, startle by dramatic contrast. For topiary is essentially personal; with it the gardener can introduce elements of individuality, even humour, into the design of the garden.

PLANTS FOR FORMAL HEDGING

Almost any kind of tree or shrub planted in a row will make a hedge. Many species, however, are grown for their flowers or berries, without which they are visually undistinguished; most such plants are suitable only for informal hedges allowed to grow with no restraint other than annual pruning of flowered shoots or dead wood. This excludes from discussion here plants such as lilac, daphne or broom, each reliable for lax, informal hedges but none responding kindly to trimming. Other species, such as *Pyracantha coccinea* or *Berberis darwinii*, though they will make a neat clipped hedge, cannot be expected to flower profusely or bear a good crop of berries, since regular clipping inevitably removes most flowering wood.

Amongst remaining plants commonly used for hedging are evergreen shrubs with large leaves, such as spotted laurel or Japanese aucuba (*Aucuba japonica*), Portugal laurel (*Prunus lusitanica*) or rhododendron, all pruned to shape with secateurs (hand pruners) to avoid the unsightly die-back of cut leaves. While a hedge of these is useful as a wind-break or imposing background for other plants, it will occupy a lot of room and can only be clipped to a semi-formal finish. In smaller gardens a hedge of these spreading species would be hopelessly out of scale.

For colour and shelter from wind all the year round small-leaved evergreens are ideal. Amongst these the shrubby honeysuckle, *Lonicera nitida*, and various forms of privet (which tends to be deciduous in exposed situations and colder climatic zones) were once great favourites. In recent years, however, they have been unjustly despised, partly because both are extremely vigorous and need frequent clipping, which offends the modern fashion for avoiding work in the garden. They also succeed in poorer soils, sometimes too well in the case of privet whose roots often take nutrients from the soil to some distance each side of the hedge, to the detriment of neighbouring plants.

Privet is an outstanding survivor in heavily polluted atmospheres, but the resulting accusation that it is only useful as an urban plant is undeserved. Well-maintained, a privet hedge provides a neat and dense neutral background for other plants in any garden, while its golden form can be a highlight throughout the year. *Lonicera nitida* is a little less robust and best kept below about 150cm (5ft) high to retain its density; clipped very low it makes a vigorous substitute for box edging.

Arbor-vitae (thuja) and yew are combined in a continuous hedge at the Ladew Topiary Gardens, Maryland.

A hedge of Handsworth box will grow slowly to 240cm–3m (8–10ft), with only one or two clips annually to keep it trim. Both holm or holly oak (*Quercus ilex*) and yew are useful for screens and hedges, their sombre evergreen foliage eventually providing a uniform passive background to flowering plants. Holly is a classic tough hedging species, both for divisions within the garden and as an impenetrable boundary hedge; regular clipping, however, prevents berries from developing. The young growth of many varieties of holly is often quite distinct in colour and can be a decorative feature.

Several types of conifers are used for hedges, although with the notable exception of yew none is entirely happy when tightly trimmed, since their beauty lies emphatically in the grace and delicacy of their naturally unrestrained foliage. Leyland cypress is excessively popular because of its energetic growth, but for this very reason it looks corsetted when pruned as a hedge any lower than 3–3.5m (10–12ft) in height, nor is it easy to keep trimmed to less than about 120cm (4ft) wide. The use of cypresses is best restricted to producing tall semi-formal screens in larger gardens where the tendency for all kinds to spread and become bare at the base need not be such a visual disadvantage.

Deciduous species are among the hardiest hedging plants, although they cannot provide

Imaginative use can be made of the modest privet, here clipped into dramatic pinnacles that echo the spire of a church beyond.

the same degree of winter protection for the garden as evergreens. Beech (green and copper forms) and hornbeam are particularly popular, both species tolerating formal clipping and retaining their dead leaves as an attractive winter bonus. Myrobalan or cherry plum is uncommon these days, while hawthorn tends unfortunately to be regarded as an agricultural hedging plant; both, however, can be clipped into rugged impenetrable boundaries, and when plashed or 'laid' (see p.73) have been used in the past for garden divisions where their neatly woven framework is revealed in winter like a hurdle fence.

PRACTICAL USES OF HEDGES

Unlike topiary, which is almost exclusively decorative, hedges are usually designed with a practical motive, few gardeners having either room or inclination to plant one merely as an ornamental addition to the garden. Although its primary function may be utilitarian, however, a hedge need not always be dull; as we have seen, if designed with a little imagination it can make a positive contribution to the overall impact of the garden.

Most people today plant hedges, as they have

done for centuries, to provide shelter or privacy, and above all to define the limits of their property. Ironically, this is probably the least effective use of a hedge. Where cost is an important factor in deciding how to enclose ground, a hedge will certainly prove the cheapest method especially if the area is very large. Around smaller gardens, though, hedging plants can occupy a disproportionately wider strip of ground, and require more maintenance, than a fence or wall of similar height. Within the garden a dividing hedge of beech can be trimmed to less than 30cm (1ft) wide, but for boundaries a strip of ground at least 60cm (2ft) wide and often more will be needed all round if the hedge is to give adequate privacy. This might be an extravagant use of precious space unless the hedge serves a further purpose such as sheltering the garden from wind or providing a decorative background to plants.

Take care when planting round the perimeter of the garden that a growing hedge does not encroach on ground that is not yours, or cause a nuisance either to a neighbour or to passers-by on a public highway. In practice this means planting so that the outer side of the mature hedge is still on or within your legal boundary.

Archways give sculptural form to a functional boundary hedge in Coconut Grove, Miami.

There is no legal right of trespass for the purpose of trimming a hedge or clearing the clippings.

Where a hedge is intended to be proof against intrusion it might be best to use a thorny species such as holly, berberis, hawthorn or gooseberries. Plashing (see p.73) or planting against a wire-netting fence will improve impenetrability, as will setting the plants at high density, either 15–22cm (6–9in) apart or as a double row with plants staggered 22cm (9in) apart each way. (Conifers such as cypress or *Thuja plicata* are not suitable for this purpose because their foliage tends to become too sparse at the base.)

Although less effective than fences for providing privacy, security or a barrier against noise, hedges make excellent wind-breaks that filter wind rather than obstruct its passage altogether. Evaporation of moisture from the soil is reduced, while plants are less likely to suffer damage or setbacks from cold winds. A hedge planted at right angles to the prevailing wind will give shelter on its leeward side to a distance of seven or eight times its height. Additional decorative hedges strategically sited within the garden can reinforce this effect. Be careful, however, not to plant too dense a hedge at the bottom of a sloping garden; in frosty weather this will impede the movement of cold air down hill and turn the garden into a frost trap.

SOME DECORATIVE USES OF HEDGES

Very often a hedge is planted to hide some eyesore, whether a neighbouring building or simply a compost heap in a corner of the garden. A plain, straight screen of privet or cypress is a practical solution, yet a more imaginatively planned hedge could be a decorative feature in its own right. A gently curving hedge will occupy little more room than a straight one, with perhaps a trained arch or columns framing an opening for access behind. Its foliage could be chosen to set off the colours of plants arranged in front during their flowering season, and to give continuing interest in winter during their drab dormancy.

ORNAMENTAL HEDGES

Tapestry or Mosaic Hedges

With care a number of different but compatible plants can be combined in a hedge to give a tapestry or harlequin appearance. Flowering shrubs can be used but it is difficult to keep these trimmed formally without sacrificing the blooms. Foliage plants are much more successful for clipped tapestry hedges, such as the mixture of yew, box, holly, hornbeam and beech planted at Hidcote Manor in Gloucestershire; there the arrangement of evergreen and deciduous species provides a variety of effects as seasons change. Another possibility is to

A tapestry hedge of deciduous and evergreen species makes a varied background to a formal arrangement of roses and topiary at Montreuil, France.

combine a selection of variegated or golden forms of such species as holly, euonymous, privet, box, and *Cassinia fulvida*. Subtle patterning can be achieved by simply mixing green and variegated forms of a single species, perhaps beech or *Lonicera nitida*. Take care when choosing the combination of plants that none is too vigorous; when mixing green and golden forms of the same species, in particular, bear in mind that the latter can easily be swamped by the usually more vigorous green varieties.

Serpentine Hedges

This sinuous style of hedge planting imitates the traditional 'crinkle-crankle' garden wall that used to be designed to provide shelter within each of its alcoves for slightly tender shrubs. Serpentine hedges can be dramatic features in large gardens, as at Chatsworth House in Derbyshire (see p.32), and in smaller gardens scaled-down versions could be planted along paths; this would be particularly effective using dwarf hedging species, arranging herbs or small plants in each of the alcoves. Before planting a serpentine hedge, the proposed course should be carefully measured out and marked so that it winds regularly along its length.

Pleached and Pollarded Hedges

These decorative styles of hedging normally suit only large gardens, since for full effect the trees used need to be fairly tall: at least 240cm (8ft) for pollarded trees, and sometimes higher for a pleached canopy, tunnel or stilt hedge. In most cases trees need to be specially planted for the purpose because much of their attraction depends on regular spacing and straight, even trunks and branches.

Pollarded trees can be used to produce a highly ornamental boundary to a garden. They can also be planted against a boundary wall as an unusual method of raising its height, provided access is available on both sides for clipping and training. Pleaching is a similarly valuable device for framing or emphasizing a path or perspective, especially if the lower portion of the trees is left open so that views of the adjacent garden are not obscured.

MODIFYING HEDGES

In many gardens mature hedges may be found which, since it has been customary for many years to regard hedges as passive boundaries or barriers, are no more than plain, clipped runs of foliage with little intrinsic interest. It is often worth considering how such hedges can be modified to enhance their visual value. (Old or neglected hedges are likely to be threadbare or overgrown, however, and their condition will need to be considered first; see pp.100–102.)

A plain hedge can often be transformed into a decorative garden feature without drastic alteration. Simply softening the original sharp lines of a privet or yew hedge can help to integrate it with the rest of an informal garden. Instead of cutting the top level, consider leaving it higher in the middle and either cutting it into flat sloping faces pitched like a roof, or rounding the surface from the high centre down to each side.

The outline could be modified further by cutting the top to undulate softly and irregularly along its length. This is particularly effective with broad, established yew hedges, whose sides can be trimmed with similar freedom; even when relaxed to this extent, they still retain their dignity and the feeling of permanence typical of old gardens. Conversely, hedges with irregular outlines, whether from design or merely careless clipping, take only a couple of seasons to train into a formal shape (see pp.101–102).

Where an overgrown hedge is to be cut back to narrower dimensions, consider leaving small sections at regular intervals protruding from the rest of the hedge. Either trim them neatly like buttresses — architectural features which add visual punctuation as well as stability to a long hedge — or encourage their growth outwards to involve the hedge with the rest of the garden and suggest shallow compartments separating different combinations of plants from each other. Or you could cut a doorway or window as a clair-voyée to reveal a glimpse of the garden or view beyond.

Instead of being kept uniform, the top of a privet, yew or box hedge could be surmounted with abstract decoration such as battlements or small gable roofs, or strong vertical shoots might be retained for training into topiary shapes (see p.79). Another way to decorate the top of a plain hedge, once popular but rare today, is to graft contrasting varieties of the same species or family on to strong vertical shoots of the hedge plants, and allow the grafts to grow above the hedge as specimen trees, perhaps clipped to form mop-head standards. Silver or gold variegated forms of holly are often grafted normally by nurserymen on to more vigorous common-holly root stocks, and this practice could be extended to decorate a hedge of this species. In the same way cottagers many years ago used to graft dessert varieties of plum on to shoots of a myrobalan hedge, pears on to flowering quince and even medlars on to hawthorn. The easiest way to graft all these examples is by the method known as budding (see p.85).

PARTERRES AND KNOT GARDENS

A parterre (from the French for 'flowerbed') was historically a separate formal section of the garden, divided into a balanced pattern of beds in geometrical shapes surrounded by a wall or dwarf clipped hedge. Garden designers today use the expression more loosely to describe any ordered pattern of beds arranged to form a visible overall design uninterrupted by tall plants or irregular features. In this sense numerous suburban front gardens with beds of summer flowers are parterres.

The knot garden is an older and specifically English concept using a single bed or pattern of beds, each laid out to contain an intricate design of dwarf hedges. Sometimes the hedging was made from a single species as a framework for coloured gravel, herbs or flowering plants grown in the enclosed spaces, but often the various strands of the design were themselves contrasted by using hedging plants with different coloured or textured foliage.

The dwarf box 'Suffruticosa' provides the framework of a traditional parterre in Savannah, Georgia.

Both simple parterres and the more complex knot gardens can be used as unconventional decoration within otherwise unbroken two-dimensional expanses of lawn, courtyard or level open garden. They need not be large: size is less important than simplicity and a clear balanced design that can be enjoyed in its entirety from all angles. To look well, this style of garden needs regular, almost loving attention — and as the plants are low, will involve a lot of bending — but in return it provides a uniquely elegant and ordered centrepiece that can succeed in both modern and traditional garden contexts.

Plants used to edge parterres or for the component threads of knot gardens need to be naturally dwarf or slow-growing, and tolerant of formal clipping — a shaggy uneven outline to a knot counters the whole purpose of creating a sharply defined symmetrical pattern. The dwarf box variety 'Suffruticosa' with bright shiny green leaves is the classic species used and is still valuable provided it is given time to reach its final required height, which may be anything from 15 to 76cm (6 to 30in) according to the scale of the design. Silver, golden and darker green varieties are available for use as contrasting sections of a box knot.

Since the dainty-leaved *Lonicera nitida* grows notoriously fast it will produce a finished hedge much sooner than box and is equally attractive. But whereas box will need only one, perhaps two, clips a year, *L. nitida* must be trimmed every month if it is to keep its formal lines during the growing season. The shiny, rich-green wall germander has often been used for hedging around and within herb gardens, and requires only infrequent trimming, as does the silvery grey cotton lavender.

Short varieties of ordinary lavender can also be restrained as semi-formal flowering hedges; they will in fact benefit from being clipped at least once a year because this prevents bushes from sprawling and losing their lower foliage. If the flowers are not considered important a lavender hedge will stand being trimmed more often to keep its outline more precise. Rosemary, thyme and hyssop can be treated similarly; the short clippings can be dried and used in cooking or for pot-pourri mixtures.

Using a combination of hedging plants with contrasting foliage, a highly attractive knot can be 'tied' with several different strands which, since all these plants retain their leaves, provide a pattern of colour all year round. Corners of the design can be embellished with topiary.

PLANTS FOR TOPIARY

To give a clean, even finish when clipped, species to be worked into topiary must have small leaves, dense growth and an ability to recover quickly from clipping. Where plants are to be trained, whether as freestanding specimens or as espaliers, a further necessary characteristic is the production of long, flexible growth that can be bent and tied to training wires.

Since topiary depends for impact on its tidy appearance all year round, choice is concentrated on evergreens. Yew and box are the plants commonly associated today with topiary in British gardens. Traditionally, however, the most popular subject for the art in cottage gardens was privet, partly because so many topiary examples were created as an integral part of an existing garden hedge, which itself was often made from privet.

The extensive collection of topiary maintained at Green Animals Garden, Rhode Island, demonstrates how well privet lends itself to carving into elaborate solid figures. There the great majority of the eighty sculptured topiary figures — ranging from traditional peacocks and

A classic topiary plant, yew lends itself to both complex and simple topiary forms. Its dark, matt foliage also makes it a perfect foil for other colours and textures.

spirals to such unusual subjects as a camel, a lion and even an elephant — are made from green or golden oval-leaved or California privet (*Ligustrum ovalifolium*).

When it is regularly clipped, the strictly deciduous privet usually remains evergreen, except in harsh winters or the colder climatic zones. However, as topiary it has several disadvantages, as the Superintendent at Green Animals concedes. Maintenance requirements are high: young privet topiary in good health there often needs clipping every two weeks in summer, whereas two or three trims are sufficient to keep yew specimens in good shape all season.

Privet is not as hardy as yew, nor does it live for as long. It is also more likely to suffer local damage during a severe winter from frost, and after snow or high winds. Nevertheless, in sheltered gardens some of the more distinguished species and cultivars of privet (see *Plant Reference Section* pp. 106–122) can still be valuable fast-growing plants for sculptured topiary, especially where a hedge of this material already exists. The naturally twiggy growth habit makes it a less satisfactory medium for trained topiary.

For this the flexible shoots of yew are ideal. The species is very hardy and responds readily to intricate training and hard pruning, even well back into old wood which quickly reclothes itself with foliage. Although slow to develop in comparison with privet, for example, young established plants can put on 30cm (12in) of new growth each year, so that smaller pieces of topiary will begin to take shape four or five years after planting, while larger examples look respectable after ten.

The tree traditionally cultivated for topiary in Mediterranean regions is the cypress, *Cupressus sempervirens*, unfortunately too tender to be reliably hardy in most of Britain or in colder regions of the USA. Even when apparently established in mild gardens, quite mature specimens often die unexpectedly from sudden or unseasonal frosts. Where Mediterranean cypress can be planted with confidence, it remains a favourite medium for simple architectural topiary on account of its solid rapid growth and tolerance of regular clipping.

Box is another traditional plant for topiary, both the naturally dwarf edging box, 'Suffruticosa', which is ideal for small work up to about

The Mediterranean cypress, popular in the gardens of Ancient Rome, is one of the earliest recorded topiary plants. Its use, however, is limited to warmer regions, as here in the south of France.

75cm (30in) and the more vigorous Handsworth box for large pieces 3–3.5m (10–12ft) tall. It is better sculpted rather than trained, as is *Lonicera nitida*, valuable for small topiary less than 1m (3ft) high; above this size bushes are prone to bareness at their base.

The dense, glossy-leaved *Phillyrea angustifolia* and *Osmanthus decora* can both be clipped into simple shapes up to about 180cm (6ft) high. Although rarely planted today, they were popular subjects for topiary a century or two ago, as were *Rhamnus alaternus*, like holly and privet well suited to urban gardens where atmospheric pollution might be a problem; *Juniperus communis*, a hardy slow-growing conifer that can be clipped into a freestanding shape up to about 180cm (6ft) high; and *Thuja occidentalis*, green in summer but often turning bronze in cold winters. Thuja is a popular topiary plant in the USA, as is ivy, the latter trained over wire frames into elaborate shapes.

The virtues and disadvantages of these, and other less commonly used species, are listed in the *Plant Reference Section* (pp. 106-122).

TOPIARY DESIGN

A garden is primarily a place in which to indulge your own personal taste. Included in that is the choice of topiary subjects. Despite the critics, who frequently advise that topiary should be confined to sober and restrained shapes, avoiding anything unusual or eccentric that might involve 'cutting and torturing trees into all sorts of fantastic shapes', to quote one nineteenth-century authority, a place can usually be found for the most bizarre work of topiary. Because it is made from a living plant, it will tend to blend with its surroundings far more easily than many examples of garden statuary.

Although the topiary in many surviving famous gardens is limited to architectural shapes such as cones, pyramids, cylinders or tetrahedrons, this formality is no more than a legacy from passing fashion. A much earlier tradition revelled in representations of animals, birds, churches and other fanciful 'conceits', providing a sound historical precedent for modern topiary ships and armchairs.

Geometrical and architectural forms are generally most satisfying when used as part of a balanced design in large or formal gardens, and lend themselves less to use as specimen topiary in small domestic gardens. Here, it is often best to use them to decorate the ends of an existing clipped hedge or a corner where two hedges meet, leaving some of the growth untrimmed until there is enough to shape into a column, a finial or perhaps a ball surmounting the hedge. Only occasionally in such gardens does a position invite the use of a lone obelisk or sphere.

Birds and animals are favourite subjects, trained on top of hedges or on the ground with a separate bush planted for each leg. With these naturalness, not symmetry, is important. Paired peacocks might be shaped in different, answering poses rather than mirror each other. The head of an animal like a dog or fox might lean to one side, or be raised in alarm or to sniff the wind. Think how the subject moves. Study photographs and then simplify a typical position to be recreated in topiary by the appropriate method. For an alert subject such as a prowling cat or a stoat, it will be most effective to shape the topiary by pulling or wiring stems into position for heads, tails or limbs, which will give the figures a greater feeling of tension; carving to shape is a technique more suited to creating fat, comfortable doves.

With any topiary design, simplicity is essential: the more complicated it is, the sooner its outlines become blurred by new growth and need redefining. The same caution applies to

planning a collection of topiary. Do not overcrowd the canvas by gathering too many separate and different examples close to each other; and if there is room to plant several, consider relating them to each other as a coherent group.

There is now a great need to find a modern idiom in topiary, rather than to carry on imitating traditional forms. A few enterprising gardeners have created battleships or riders on horseback, and certainly the medium lends itself to such abstract design as Cubist 'cloud' pruning or the Baroque stylized reliefs at the Villa Garzoni (see opposite). As yet, however, few of the forms of modern art have found their way into topiary, even though many of Henry Moore's works, for example, would make practical and impressive projects in yew, privet or Handsworth box. Gardeners still have plenty of scope for experiment.

Below: A touch of fantasy has transformed a yew hedge into a ramshackle topiary house at Westwell Manor in Oxfordshire.
Opposite: The free forms of topiary in the seventeenth-century garden at the Villa Garzoni in Tuscany can still offer inspiration for modern design.

PLANTING

SELECTION AND SITING OF PLANTS

Many gardeners these days buy on impulse, when a plant strategically displayed in a garden centre happens to catch their fancy. Such spontaneous decisions are fine where herbaceous plants or some of the smaller shrubs are concerned; most of these are reasonably tolerant of being moved around the garden, even several times until the best position is found. However, this impromptu approach could be disastrous when buying topiary material. Unless they are to be grown in pots or tubs that can be relocated without disturbing their contents, these plants should be selected with care, and sited where they can settle down and flourish for many years. Once they are any size it will be difficult, although not impossible (see pp.102–103), to move them without setback.

Before choosing a single species or variety to grow, it is important to fix on an appropriate site and to consider environmental factors such as the climate and condition of the soil, as well as practicalities such as the labour involved and access required. All these may well influence your final decision.

Position

A leisurely look around the garden will reveal distinct variations in the performance of existing plants according to their position. Consider the effect of light. Some plants only do their best in full sun, refusing to flower if grown in shade. Others can tolerate varying degrees of shade; even so they will often look different according to the amount of sunlight they actually receive. Plants in the shade of buildings or walls, for example, tend to grow taller than in the open garden because they are drawn upwards to the light (and sometimes also as a result of the shelter the wall gives them from wind). If the shade is too heavy they may become unnaturally tall and leggy, or lean dramatically away from the wall to reach the light.

Colours also vary according to exposure to light. Evergreens planted in intermittent or light shade often keep a deeper, richer colour than when grown in full sun. Leaf variegations tend

A simple umbrella of foliage sets off the sinuous structure of a mature yew, at Bickleigh Castle, Devon.

to be more pronounced in the open, whereas shade will often emphasize the green colour of the foliage.

It can be seen, then, that where a hedge runs from deep shade into full sunlight, it may not grow uniformly, and there may be noticeable differences in colour between each end. In extreme shade some of the lower leaves and side shoots may die, especially if that section also receives little rain. To some extent it is possible to compensate for these variations by adjusting fertilizers, watering or trimming, but to achieve maximum uniformity it would be as well to plan for even exposure to light.

Shade will affect specimen topiary similarly. Ensure that the most important features of the design face the sun; there they will show to best advantage, and the faster growth will make it easier to restore any damage that might occur.

When choosing a site for plants it is just as important to remember the activity taking place below ground as that above. Most gardeners appreciate the dangers of planting vigorous shrubs or trees where their roots could damage the foundations of buildings or penetrate drains. Their effect on neighbouring plants is less often considered. All hedge plants will compete with the plants around them for water and nutrients. In this respect dwarf species are less culpable than taller plants, which will also shade others in their vicinity. Some, however, among which privet is the most notorious, have such a dense surface root system that surrounding life is starved out of existence. Be prepared to feed plants generously if they grow near such a hedge, or choose less greedy species (for example, osmanthus, berberis or cotoneaster).

Climate

The most obvious climatic limitation to the choice of plants is their frost-hardiness. This is extremely difficult to define in anything other than very general terms because regional variations are widespread and often eccentric. California in particular is notable as a patchwork of different climates and growing conditions, also the west coast of Scotland, where the climate is tempered by the warm Gulf Stream and plants grow freely that further south and inland would promptly succumb to frost.

Snow covers the formal Yew Terrace at Parnham House, Dorset. Although liable to superficial frost damage in very cold regions, yews are among the hardiest topiary plants.

Conditions can also vary noticeably between individual gardens. Even the garden itself will have its own peculiar microclimate, with sheltered spots, dry areas and frost pockets. If it is close to the sea, salt-laden winds could injure or even destroy some species; on the other hand, the influence of the sea can regularly raise minimum winter temperatures above those experienced inland, allowing slightly more tender plants to survive.

Other Criteria
Most of the specimen topiary seen today is fashioned from yew; low formal hedges are commonly of box, taller ones of yew or holly. Historical records, however, testify to the use of numerous other plants for topiary, and to these might be added yet more which will tolerate close clipping.

Although the *Plant Reference Section* (pp.106-122) does not exhaust the wide range of potential candidates, many more species are included than the conservative selection generally used for topiary and hedges in modern gardens. When choosing plants, be adventurous. An essential element of topiary is showmanship,

and there is scope for the imaginative cultivation of many species.

Choice will inevitably be influenced by factors of scale and arrangement in the overall garden design, as well as climate and site. Also, since all plants are not suitable for all functions, it will be guided by the qualities and behaviour of each species and variety. Visit gardens and assess the possibilities in the light of what you have seen, bearing in mind some of the following practical points.

Function. Although topiary exists in its own right as a form of garden sculpture, hedges are rarely solely ornamental. Usually they will also serve to mark boundaries, either merely definitive or providing in addition privacy or shelter from wind, a screen to hide an unwanted view or a barrier against intruders. Inevitably certain plants are better than others for these purposes.

Height. Consider the eventual height required and choose plants accordingly. It is hard to keep species such as *Lonicera nitida* tidy and solid above about 120cm (4ft). Box exists in several varieties with distinct characteristics: 'Suffruticosa' is naturally dwarf and seldom flourishes above 90cm (3ft), whereas 'Handsworthensis' is vigorous enough to be used for topiary up to about 3m (10ft) tall. Remember also that a tree that is now small may in the future block light from your window or a neighbour's.

Labour. Consider the amount of maintenance involved in keeping plants neat. Privet, for example, will require at least monthly clipping during the growing season, whereas yew needs only a main trim in summer and occasionally another in autumn. Clippings need to be cleared, which can be an uncomfortable job with holly, berberis or pyracantha. Bear in mind at the same time that access will be needed, perhaps several times in one season, for clipping and clearing debris.

BUYING PLANTS

When buying plants for topiary and hedging, a lot of future labour, and possible loss, can be avoided if only the best quality specimens are selected.

Garden Centres

Garden centres are often the best places to inspect and buy specimen plants to train as topiary, although they are certainly not the most economical sources for large numbers of hedging plants. Not all garden centres conscientiously maintain high standards and the quality of stock varies. It is important therefore to know what to look for when buying.

Mature yew topiary towers over a small garden. Careful thought must be given to the siting of topiary that might grow to such proportions.

Size. Topiary can take several years to mature and it is tempting to buy the largest specimens available to reduce the waiting time between planting and the finished creation. This seldom works in practice. Young, small trees adapt more readily to their new home, rooting and growing faster, so that in time they will often overtake larger trees that are still struggling.

Older plants will require more attention to staking and aftercare. There is a greater risk of losing individual trees, for example, if a hedge is planted with 2m (6ft) specimens of yew, than with trees 120cm (4ft) high which, with care, will establish more easily and catch up in width and height over two or three years. Plants only 45–60cm (18in–2ft) tall will take longer still but undoubtedly have the greatest eventual success rate. Moreover, if a bad season follows planting, large trees can be under so much stress that parts die back; these would then have to be pruned back to a balanced shape before further training.

The safest option is to buy the smallest healthy plants between one and three years old, which will usually start to grow straight away with little check.

Top growth. Generally it is important to look for symmetrical shape, whether the plants are needed for hedging or topiary; a year or two can be wasted simply correcting lop-sided growth. Hedging plants should be bushy with several side shoots evenly distributed down to near ground level. If you want plants to gain height quickly, make sure that each has a distinct and undamaged central shoot, or 'leader'.

Check the size and colour of the foliage. Unusually small leaves are a symptom of starvation, as sometimes are yellowing leaves, although this might indicate over- or underwatering instead. Frost and very cold winds will cause brown scorch-marks on the foliage of evergreens and variegated plants. All the top growth should be free from pests — some, such as scale insects, may prove difficult to eradicate later — and from obvious signs of disease, such as mildews and fungal infections.

Root growth. Even if staff protest, insist on knocking plants carefully from their containers to inspect the health of their roots. Sometimes you need not go this far: weeds on the surface of the compost usually indicate that the plant has had time to become established in its pot, whereas clean, loosely heaped compost may indicate recent potting and will most likely fall away from the roots during planting. Long, thick roots growing from the base of the container can mean the plant is root-bound.

An early stage in the development of a parterre: the dwarf box plants, about three or four years' old, are already well established, with a season's bushy growth ready for clipping.

Inside the pot, ensure that the compost is evenly moist and that a network of roots has penetrated to the sides and bottom of the root ball without girdling the base in search of more room. As a very rough guide, healthy roots are usually pale, crisp and moist, in contrast to dark and wiry or brittle dead ones; patches of these might show that the plant has been neglected at some stage. Check for pests and disease (see pp.104–105). Reject specimens with white, fluffy concentrations of root aphis, or the fat grubs of vine weevils. Pale granules mixed evenly in the compost are most likely to be perlite or another mineral additive, while small fragile spheres, suspiciously like slug and snail eggs, are often only granules of slow-release fertilizer.

Nurseries

Many nurseries, both general and specialized, supply container-grown plants in addition to their more traditional field-grown stocks, and the same criteria apply to these as to plants from garden centres. If, however, you are buying large specimens or a quantity of hedging plants you will probably be offered bare-root or balled plants. Where possible, try to visit nurseries during the growing season when you can discuss your site and choice with someone knowledgeable, and possibly see examples of mature plants. An order can then be placed for delivery sometime between October and the end of March when the plants are dormant.

Unpack the plants as soon as they arrive and check their quality and condition. Bare-root plants should have a good mass of fibrous roots in addition to their thick main roots which will probably have been cut when they were dug up; any that are torn or damaged can be trimmed clean when planting. Do not unwrap balled roots to inspect them; you will only do more harm by disturbing them.

Inspect the tops of plants for damage. Minor breakage in transit can usually be ignored, but notify the nursery promptly if there is serious injury, or if you are dissatisfied with the quality of the plants. Should you have to do this, stand plants in a shed or sheltered corner and keep the roots moist with a covering of peat or damp sacking until the nursery makes a reply to your complaint.

Plants in Bulk
If you are considering buying fifty or more hedging plants, container-grown specimens from a garden centre or nursery will be prohibitively expensive unless you can negotiate a special discount. Savings of 75 per cent or more can often be made by going to a wholesale nursery. Some who supply landscape firms will have large trees available; others supply the trade with the kind of small plants which will establish quickly in the garden.

Know what you want in advance and be specific when making enquiries — few wholesalers have either the time or expertise to advise on the choice of plants. You should also be prepared to collect your plants; since these might be bare-root, have the planting site ready in advance and take some plastic bags and damp newspapers with you to protect them on the journey.

TECHNICAL TERMS USED BY NURSERIES

Catalogues often describe stock in technical terms unintelligible to many gardeners. Below are some of the most common.

Ball; soil ball; root ball — the mass of soil around the roots, always intact on good *container-grown* plants, but often washed off *field-grown* plants, especially when these are dispatched by post.

Balled — a *field-grown* plant whose root ball has been wrapped intact in sacking (burlap).

Bare-root stock — *field-grown* plants whose roots have been shaken or washed free from soil.

Clones — plants reproduced by cuttings or layering from a common parent and therefore identical to each other.

Container-grown stock — plants grown and established in pots or plastic bags.

Cultivar — short for 'cultivated variety', a distinct variant of a species either bred purposely or arising naturally as a sport, and maintained only in cultivation, usually as a *clone*.

Feather — young side shoot on current year's growth. A *feathered* tree has not had these removed.

Field-grown — plants raised in the open ground and supplied either *balled* or *bare-root*. These must be lifted and planted while dormant.

Liner — a very young plant, either a *pot liner* or *bare-root liner*, normally needing to be grown on before sale or final potting.

Transplant — a young plant that has been moved to open ground from its nursery bed to encourage fibrous root growth. Often denoted by the abbreviations 1+1, 2+0, 1+2 etc. The first figure gives the number of years spent in the nursery bed, the second, the number of years since transplanting.

Variety — a variant within a species occurring naturally in the wild and which comes true from seed. The term is often loosely, and incorrectly, used by gardeners to indicate a *cultivar*.

Whip — a young unpruned tree.

PROPAGATION

Many old hedges and topiary trees were not originally bought as plants but started life as seeds or cuttings. Certainly cottage gardeners in the past would have been unable to afford expensive nursery stock and instead they either transferred stray seedlings to their gardens or started plants themselves. Propagating your own is still the cheapest way to obtain plants or increase your stock, and often the only way to make sure they are identical with varieties already growing in the garden. There is enormous satisfaction, too, in having produced your own plants.

(The best methods of propagating hedge and topiary plants are indicated according to species in the *Plant Reference Section* pp. 106–122.)

Seeds

Provided good seed can be obtained, this is often the easiest method of raising a large quantity of plants, although it usually takes the longest time and results can be variable. Hedges made of yew grown from seed, for example, may have distinct patches of different shades of green; to avoid this it is necessary to use plants struck as cuttings from a common parent (clones).

Bought seed is usually reliable because it will

The billowing shape of this old box hedge seems to have evolved over years of informal clipping. Traditionally, such hedges sprang from seedlings or cuttings propagated by cottage gardeners.

have been tested for viability. Home-saved seed must be gathered fully ripe from healthy parents and either sown immediately or stored in cool, slightly moist surroundings, preferably in plastic bags in a refrigerator. Where appropriate, sow outdoors in the autumn to take advantage of freshness and the action of frost to break natural dormancy and trigger germination.

Prepare a small bed where seedlings can stay undisturbed if necessary for two years. Weed the ground thoroughly and cultivate it to fine tilth. Space the seeds evenly in straight lines for ease of weeding, and water them using a fine rose whenever dry. While some precocious seedlings will need to be transplanted a year later, others will progress more slowly and can spend a further year in the seed bed.

Alternatively sow thinly in soil-based compost in a greenhouse or cold frame, using pans for fine seeds, deep trays for larger ones. Transplant when large enough, either into trays or after hardening off to a nursery bed outdoors.

Layering

This method of propagation is almost foolproof since it depends on the natural tendency of many plants to root wherever a side shoot touches the ground. The shoot stays joined to the parent plant until it can rely on its own roots for sustenance. Sometimes there is no need to sever it: gaps in lavender hedges, for example, can be filled by layering side shoots that remain attached although themselves rooted in place. An area of ivy on a wall can be encouraged to extend sideways if one or two long shoots are layered on each side. For bulk propagation, several suitably placed branches can be layered around a large plant and most will be ready for transfer a year later.

Shoots for layering need to be healthy, flexible so that they bend without breaking, and long enough to reach the ground comfortably some distance from their tips. First, expose the green tissues inside the shoot where it will touch the ground. This can be done in three ways: by cutting the shoot obliquely to about half-way through and then keeping the split open either with a matchstick or by bending the shoot back; by skinning off a strip of the bark; or by simply twisting a thin shoot gently to tear through the bark. Keeping the wound in contact with the soil, hold the shoot in place with a stone or peg it with a loop of strong wire, and cover the rooting area with a small mound of friable soil. If a young plant with an upright stem is required, tie the end of the shoot vertically to a cane. When the layer is well rooted, water and then separate it from its parent for planting elsewhere.

Cuttings

To be sure of success when taking cuttings from trees and shrubs it is important to distinguish between the different kinds, since some root more easily than others according to species.

Soft-wood. These are like the cuttings gardeners usually take from house plants. About 7–10cm (3–4in) long, they are cut from the soft tips of the current year's growth.

Semi-hardwood or half-ripe. These are made from slightly older wood, still less than a year old, often comprising a short shoot intact with a 'heel' or strip of bark from the stem at its base.

Both these kinds are rooted in pots filled with a proprietory brand of cutting compost or a mixture of equal parts peat and sharp sand. Insert the cuttings, stripped of their lower leaves, around the edge of the pot and water them in. Place the pot inside a plastic bag, secured at the top to keep it moist. Once they have rooted, often indicated by new growth at their tips, they can be potted up singly.

Hard-wood. These are ripe, year-old shoots about 30cm (12in) long, planted to half their depth in the open ground in autumn. If the soil is light, simply push them into the ground after removing their lower leaves. Otherwise, make a slit in the ground, fill it with old potting compost plus, on heavier soils, a bottom layer of coarse sand, and insert them into this. Gently tread the soil firm. They will usually be rooted and ready to move a year later.

Layering. **1.** *Making the incision in a suitably placed flexible side shoot.* **2.** *The prepared stem with the cut wedged open.* **3.** *The layer pegged in place and supported.*

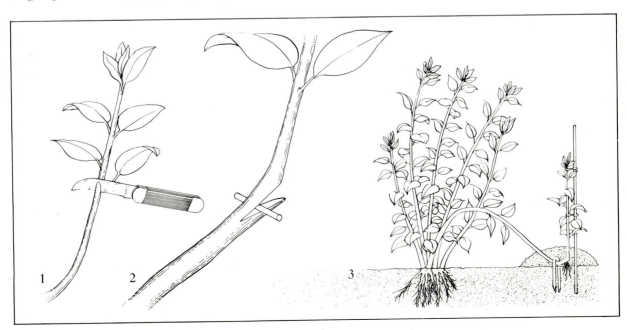

PREPARING THE GROUND

Topiary and hedging plants are permanent features in the garden and often very long-lived — some specimens of clipped box and yew, for example, are still flourishing after more than 200 years. Thus it is well worth paying some attention to soil conditions before planting.

While the individual preferences of the plants available are very varied, and a few have an aversion to particular soil types (see *Plant Reference Section* pp.106–122), the majority will be happy in any reasonably fertile and workable soil. In most gardens, only a few simple soil improvements will need to be made to give them a good start: the correction of inhospitable extremes of texture and structure by lightening heavy or sticky clays, or adding body to thin, sandy soils. Otherwise, you could be demanding too much from some species: holly, for example, often sulks in wet, heavy ground, while conifers such as spruce and hemlock do not grow well on shallow or chalky soils.

First of all it is necessary to identify the soil type in your garden. It is often advisable in addition to have a sample of soil tested for fertility and acidity — or, if you are planning a large project such as a hedge, knot garden or parterre, several samples of soil taken from different parts of the proposed site. Do-it-yourself kits can be bought inexpensively to give a rough estimate, or samples can be sent away to be analysed more closely. The results will enable you to correct excessive acidity or alkalinity of the soil and make good any nutrient deficiency well before planting — or alternatively, to choose species that prefer or at least tolerate the existing soil conditions.

Sandy Soils

Although light ground is usually a joy to work and rapidly warms up in spring, it suffers from a lack of clay or humus to hold the soil particles together. As a result the dusty surface of unimproved sandy soils tends to form a hard impermeable crust after heavy rain. Sandy soils are 'hungry' because plant foods are rapidly leached out of them, and lacking resistance to evaporation they dry early in the season, causing a consequent check to plant growth. All these deficiencies are best corrected during cultivation by working in as much organic material as possible to help retain moisture and stabilize the structure; and afterwards by regular mulching

The garden at Levens Hall, Cumbria, with its diverse collection of topiary, was first laid out in 1692.

BASIC SOIL TYPES

Sand — gritty, pours between fingers and does not stain the hand. Rare; much more common is:

Sandy loam — cannot be moulded, has a gritty texture and will mark fingers.

Medium loam — the ideal; has an open, granular texture, can be squeezed into a ball which readily falls apart again.

Clay loam — greasy and easily moulded into a ball, which disintegrates when dropped. Not as sticky as:

Clay — can be moulded and polished between fingers like plasticine or putty. Very sticky.

---

which adds nutrients and protects the soil against drying out — a potential catastrophe if it occurs during the first season or two.

Heavy Soils

These are more often a problem for gardeners, since no amount of arduous digging seems to tame them. Not only are heavy soils hard to work, but they remain cold until late in the season. Even worse is their tendency to lie wet, which can cause stagnation at the roots. However, most clay soils are inherently very fertile, and the main task with these is to improve their workability by physically opening up their structure, traditionally by a system of drainage and/or by adding coarse humus. Subsequent mulching will protect the surface from its typical seasonal variation between sticky mud and cracked concrete.

Clay can also be broken down with mineral top-dressing, although this is not a substitute for thorough preliminary cultivation. A mixture by volume of 80 per cent gypsum and 20 per cent dolomite is scattered in autumn on the soil surface at the rate of 125g per sq m (4oz per sq yd), and either hoed in or left for rains to wash into the soil. On very sticky soils repeat the dressing in spring. Thereafter a single annual application should be enough to maintain improved friability without increasing the alkalinity. (Note that most so-called clay busters or improvers are only expensive adaptations of this mixture. Also, a large bag of gypsum or dolomite from a farm supplier costs very little more than a small carton of either mineral from a garden centre.)

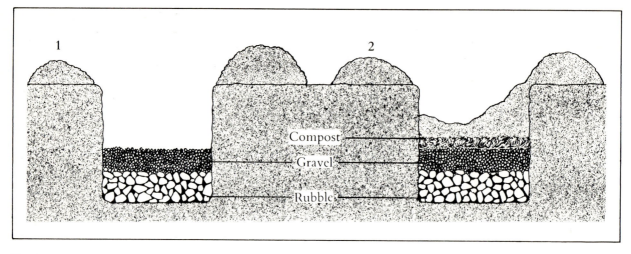

Drainage

When heavy soils remain waterlogged, or where a clay subsoil prevents surface water from clearing, it may be necessary to consider improving the drainage. In extreme cases the whole garden would probably benefit from a professionally laid system of land drains. Most gardeners, fortunately, need concentrate only on particular planting sites.

For specimen trees, excavate any good topsoil from an area about 1m (1yd) square and then break up the subsoil with a fork, working into it gravel or small stones from around the garden, together with any turf stripped from the surface, garden compost or other rough organic material. Ideal for this is the fibrous mixture of leaves and small twigs raked up in autumn and usually wasted on the bonfire.

When cultivating heavy ground for a hedge, prepare the whole row in similar fashion, as a strip rather than individual sites. In very bad cases dig out a deep trench along the proposed course, leading to a soakaway constructed beyond one end of the hedge. Fill the bottom of the trench with a thin layer of rubble before returning the soil, improved as below, to leave a raised ridge which will help shed surface water. Never simply replace excavated clay with a potting or planting compost, since this pocket of very porous soil creates in effect a soakaway in which water from the surrounding ground will collect.

Soil Preparation

Whatever the condition of the ground it is best to dig two spits (spade-depths) deep and to break up the soil as thoroughly as possible. For specimen trees prepare about 1 sq m (1 sq yd) of ground; for a hedge cultivate a strip 90–120cm (3–4ft) wide, extending 60–90cm (2–3ft) beyond each end. Mix in at least a bucketful of organic material per sq m (yd), preferably twice this,

Drainage trench for hedge planting in heavy ground.
1. Drainage materials placed in the bottom of the trench.
2. Compost and topsoil laid above.

using very old manure, rotted leaves, garden compost or peat, plus a 12cm (5in) potful of bonemeal. A proprietory tree-planting compost containing a slow-release feed could be used in place of both humus and bonemeal, but it is considerably more expensive and would be uneconomical for a hedging trench. There is little point adding chemical fertilizers at this stage since most will be washed out before the plants can use them.

This work is ideally carried out the autumn before spring planting; where this is not practicable, however, try to leave as much time as possible between preparation and planting, to allow the freshly turned soil to settle.

Weeds

It is far easier to clear weeds before planting than afterwards. If time allows and you have no objection to using weedkillers, treat the planting area when the weeds are in active growth with a total herbicide such as glyphosate or ammonium sulphamate. Planting can follow as soon as a week after the use of glyphosate, or between six weeks and three months later if ammonium sulphamate has been used; but ensure that the dead weed growth has been cleared or dug in first.

The non-chemical alternative is to skim off any turf with a spade, saving it to bury during cultivation. Fork out the weeds, trying to remove most of the root fragments from such perennials as ground elder, couch grass and bindweed. Some will inevitably slip through to grow again later, but it should be possible to fork them out after planting the shrubs, or to spot-treat them with weedkiller. A black plastic mulch (see p.59) can if necessary be used to prevent their regrowth.

PLANTING PROCEDURE

Timing
It is tempting to assume that container-grown trees and shrubs can be planted with success at any time of the year. Although with care this is possible, planting during the summer demands close attention to regular watering for the rest of the season to avoid injury to the unestablished root ball from drought. Despite advice to the contrary, it is still wisest to plant most subjects between autumn and spring to prevent any unnecessary stress when they are actively growing. Never plant when the ground is sodden from heavy rain, nor when it is frozen.

Plant bare-rooted subjects according to the appropriate season: between leaf-fall and the end of March for deciduous plants, from October until May for evergreens. Within these limits it is better to wait for comfortable weather and soil conditions outdoors than to plant in haste to any deadline.

If the weather is unfavourable when they arrive, line out open-ground plants in a trench, and heel them in by covering the roots with soil trodden firmly into place. Container-grown plants should be stood in a sheltered part of the garden where they are secure from winds; move them under cover if severe frost threatens.

Planting
Dig out a hole in the prepared ground somewhat wider than the root ball so that there is room to spread the roots comfortably. As a general rule of thumb, the hole should be dug twice as wide as the root ball and one and a half times as deep; it will then be necessary to back-fill to bring the plant to ground level — in the case of bare-rooted plants, aligned to the soil line on its stem. Test the roots in the hole for size and, where necessary, drive in any stakes before planting.

A few hours prior to planting, thoroughly water containers. Cleanly trim any broken or torn roots on open-ground plants and then soak them in a bucket of water. Tap container-grown plants from their pots or, if they are in black plastic liners, slit open the plastic with a knife, in either case taking care the root ball does not disintegrate. If larger plants have their roots balled in sacking, first place them in their holes and then cut the material, leaving the portion beneath the plant in place if its removal would disturb the roots. There is no need to loosen the roots of container-grown plants unless they are pot-bound and wrapped round at the base, in which case they should be gently unravelled and laid to radiate evenly from the plant to encourage their outward growth.

With the plant in place, refill the hole with well broken soil, checking as you go that it is still upright — except in the case of hedges, where slender specimens (such as rooted but unbranched cuttings) are better planted leaning at an angle so that the top of one overlaps the base of the next. Work the soil with your fingers between any loose roots. When the hole is half filled, firm around the plant with your foot without compacting the soil too heavily. Repeat this when the hole is filled, then lightly loosen and level the surface around the stem.

The fine roots on open-ground plants rapidly dry out, especially in sunny or windy weather, when half an hour's exposure can cause irreparable damage. When several bare-rooted specimens are to be planted, take them one at a time, leaving the rest in a shaded place and covered with a damp sack or moist organic matter, or soaking in a bucket of water.

The ideal time to plant any tree or shrub is during mild, showery conditions, when the soil is moist but not too wet to handle, and when further rainfall is likely to settle the replaced soil around the roots. Gardeners, however, generally prefer to work in dry weather, and in most cases this will mean watering in the shrubs during and after planting. Use a hose or a watering can with a rose (spray) to ensure even saturation, otherwise dry soil around the plants will absorb all the water.

Container-grown shrubs should be thoroughly soaked before planting, and watered again as soon as they are in the ground. Bare-rooted plants, and also any that are planted close to a wall, are best 'puddled in'. Prepare the planting hole to the appropriate size and depth, including plenty of moisture-retentive humus during soil preparation to provide a valuable reservoir of water below ground. Stand the shrub in place and fill the hole with water. When the water has drained away, refill with the excavated soil and firm as usual. Water again after planting.

In very dry conditions, plant during the evening and then water with a sprinkler left to run for a couple of hours.

(For planting topiary in tubs and containers, on banks and against walls, see pp.62–67.)

Support
Most taller specimen trees, especially evergreens, will benefit during their early years from the support of stakes driven in on the side facing the prevailing wind. After planting, secure each plant to its stake, using either a proprietory adjustable tree tie or string looped around a sacking collar.

Where trees are to be trained with twisting 'barleysugar' stems, a cylindrical pole should be used for support so that there are no angles or irregularities in its growth. Stakes with a square section are preferable, however, for topiary specimens whose side shoots need training along armatures; these are more readily kept in the correct plane if nailed to a flat-sided stake.

Protection

Early growth can be accelerated in all gardens, but especially in those exposed to cold or drying winds, if a temporary wind-break is erected for the first two or three seasons. A solid fence is not a good structure for this purpose because it would have a tendency to force plants, leading to spindly growth with sparse foliage at the base. Plastic mesh netting that allows about half the wind to filter through has been found to give the best results: several kinds are marketed for

'Barleysugar' stems can be shaped either by training the young main stem around a cylindrical stake or by winding a spiral of stout wire round the stem to hold it in shape.

the purpose. Since it will bear the brunt of strong winds this netting will need to be secured to sturdy posts.

Very small plants and trees can be enclosed on all four sides by specially designed translucent plastic guards which provide a degree of 'greenhouse' protection while allowing ventilation and watering from above. Various kinds are available, most of them increasing the temperature within by several degrees.

In gardens where rabbits are likely to be a problem it is essential to protect the stems and lower growth of newly planted trees and shrubs with spiral plastic guards that encircle the stems and expand as growth progresses.

Mulching

Top-dressing the soil with a substantial blanket of organic material after planting serves several purposes. For hedge and topiary plants, and most of all for any growing in the dry soil at the base of walls, a mulch is particularly valuable in preventing evaporation and so conserving the moisture important for rapid root establishment. Weed germination is also inhibited, reducing competition for water and nutrients. There is less fluctuation in ground temperature, and extremes of wet and dry conditions are prevented, improving stability on most soils.

A layer 5–8cm (2–3in) deep of an organic material such as old manure, mushroom compost, peat or shredded bark mulch is ideal, because these are sufficiently coarse to provide effective insulation without preventing air and water from reaching the soil; material as fine as sawdust, on the other hand, is liable to compact into an impervious layer. Grass clippings are useful, provided the lawn has not been treated recently with chemicals, although only a little (2.5cm/1in or so) should be laid at any one time to avoid overheating as the grass decays.

Spread the mulch evenly at least 45cm (18in) around the plants in all directions. Make sure the material is not packed too densely around plant stems where rot could start, and only apply a mulch when the ground is warm and moist, otherwise its insulating effects might be counterproductive, preventing rain and sunlight from reaching cold or dry soil. Most mulches will need topping up as they decay, especially grass clippings, and if the material tends to compact it should be pricked over lightly with a fork because a loose layer is best for insulation, aeration and control of weeds.

Although unattractive in appearance, an efficient weed suppressor and protective mulch is black plastic sheeting, which can be used either by cutting a slit to the centre of a piece 1m (1yd) square and then spreading this flat around the stem, or by planting through a sheet laid on moist prepared ground. In many cases it is possible to grow cuttings inserted directly through the plastic, under which they usually root much faster than in the open ground. Make sure the ground is thoroughly moist and reasonably level before laying a plastic mulch, and secure the edges by weighing them down with stones or a layer of soil, or by heeling them into slits cut in

In the knot garden at Atlanta Botanical Garden, Georgia, shredded bark mulch is used both to suppress weeds and to provide a neutral background to the clipped foliage.

the ground with a spade. Gravel can be spread over the top to conceal the plastic. Whereas an organic mulch is useful as a permanent aid to good cultivation, the value of black plastic lies primarily in encouraging rapid establishment, and after two seasons it can be removed. Beware of plastic mulches, however, in extremely hot climates or climates with high solar radiation. In these locations a plastic mulch may cause dangerously high temperatures.

In China and Japan trees are sometimes surrounded with a layer of stones laid flat on top of each other around the trunk to keep the soil below cool and moist and protected from erosion. This would be a decorative alternative method of mulching specimen trees for topiary.

Pruning

Gardeners always disagree about the virtues of pruning newly planted shrubs. Many are understandably reluctant to cut back a newly purchased plant, especially since this would seem to defeat the aim of quickly achieving the desired height and width.

Whether to prune or not depends ultimately on the purpose for which the plants are intended. If you are establishing a hedge, for example, it is often essential to cut young plants back to avoid the danger of rapid upward

growth at the expense of side shoots lower down. To concentrate energy into lateral thickening cut young deciduous hedging plants back to about half their height after planting; shorten resulting growth by half the following summer (exceptions such as beech and hornbeam are detailed in the *Plant Reference Section* pp.106–122). Treat most young evergreens (but not conifers) similarly after planting, and prune again late the next winter or early in spring.

If a hedge is being made with high-quality specimens that are already large and bushy (usually either container-grown specimens or ones that have been transplanted at the nursery), there may be no need to cut the plants back or stop their leading shoots. These, together with conifers, specimen trees for topiary and plants for raised hedges need not be pruned until they reach their final height, when the tip of the main vertical shoot, or leader, is removed. Plants that do not have a compact, fibrous root ball may suffer stress after planting unless they are cut back to compensate for root damage.

Recreation of parterre and pergola at Het Loo, Holland: hedge plants have been encouraged into bushy growth by clipping early on; the sides of the pergola have also been clipped while the top continues to be trained upwards.

AFTERCARE

Although it is important to give shrubs the best possible start by planting them correctly, it should not be assumed that they are self-sufficient thereafter. More woody plants are lost through neglect during the following season or two than from mistakes in planting. Because of their slower growth compared with herbaceous plants, for example, they take longer to establish and therefore need every encouragement to cope with adverse weather while young.

Watering

The most common cause of loss in the first season is lack of water, especially if the shrubs have been planted in spring when they will have to start growth before they can depend on the roots to support them. Once the weather turns hot and dry, they are likely to be under considerable strain unless watered regularly. Symptoms of stress are yellowing of leaves and young shoots' becoming limp, with partial or total loss of foliage and die-back in extreme cases. (The loss of a few leaves immediately after planting evergreens, however, is not usually a sign of distress, but an indication that normal growth is under way.)

Unless the weather is wet, check the soil below the surface around newly planted trees and shrubs every fortnight. If it is dry, soak the area with a sprinkler or leave a hose gently trickling at the base of each plant for a couple of hours. Alternatively give each plant three or four cans of water (23ltr/6 US gal per sq m/yd is ideal). It is important to soak the ground thoroughly, preferably in the cool of evening or early morning; light sprinklings of water quickly evaporate in hot weather and can actually be injurious by encouraging vulnerable surface rooting. Mulching plants after heavy rain, or fluffing up an existing mulch, will delay the need to start watering.

Probably during the second season, and certainly after that, plants will be able to cope with moderately dry conditions. In a very hot summer, however, be prepared to give them an occasional prolonged soaking. Specimens grown in tubs will always need regular and thorough watering to prevent the soil from drying out; once this happens, it is very difficult to evenly wet it again.

Weeds

Where plants have been mulched weeds should not be too great a problem; otherwise, take care for the first two or three seasons to prevent weeds from becoming established. Experiments have shown that young trees always grow faster when free from competition for water and soil nutrients. For this reason, even if they are eventually to be grassed down, hedges and trees should not be planted direct into turf, nor must grass be allowed to encroach until the plants are fully established.

Frost and Wind

Once established, plants will normally cope with these seasonal hazards, but during the first few months, especially if the shrubs have been planted in autumn, make sure hard frost has not disturbed the roots by heaving up the soil. If this does happen, tread the soil firm once more around the stem to prevent the roots from drying out, or replant altogether if the plant has been badly disturbed.

Similarly, check after high winds that the plants have not been blown about, and in particular that they have not rocked violently from side to side, loosening them in the ground. Specimens in tubs are often vulnerable to wind and severe frost while young; where possible try to avoid trouble by siting them where they are not too exposed. Otherwise, move them temporarily to a sheltered place or screen them from high winds. Small tubs can be wrapped in insulating material such as bubble-plastic sheeting to prevent their freezing solid. In exposed areas it is worth maintaining wind protection until the plants are obviously thriving.

Ties and Stakes

If the plants have been securely supported there will be little risk of damage from wind. However, make sure the ties have not broken nor are chafing against the stems and injuring the bark. Check regularly that ties have not become too tight for the growing stems, otherwise they will bite into the wood, cutting a permanent girdle, or even inhibit growth. Either slacken them or, if they are there merely for initial support, remove both the ties and the stakes after a couple of seasons.

Feeding

Hedges and clipped trees need feeding throughout their lives. During their formative years the plants require feeding so that they grow rapidly; once mature they still need a regular feed to encourage them to replace growth constantly removed by trimming — unless they have the benefit of growing next to a fertile, well tended bed. As with the best lawns, a fine appearance is ultimately the result of a balance between feeding and trimming.

Provided the soil has been improved before

Chestnut hedge and standard trees in formation: stakes can be removed from individual trees when well established, or retained if necessary to correct shape; weed-free conditions aid rapid growth.

planting, there should be no need to give fertilizers during the first season. However, if plants are under stress from drought, in addition to watering it is beneficial to spray them with a foliar feed to assist the hard-worked roots. After the first season, feed the plants each year, either at the start of the season or immediately after the first trim, with a balanced compound fertilizer at a rate of 125g per sq m (4oz per sq yd) evenly distributed around the plants. When they have reached their required size, halve this rate. If plants are mulched annually with a manure, there is no need to dress them with chemical fertilizers as well.

TUBS AND CONTAINERS

Choosing Containers

When planting topiary in tubs or other containers, it is important not to choose a container just for its attractive appearance, but to ensure that it is sufficiently large and resilient for permanent occupation. Unless you are prepared to repot and root-prune trees regularly, tubs must be large enough to hold a substantial volume of soil. In cold climates, relatively tender subjects such as bay and myrtle might have to be housed or moved to a more sheltered outdoor area in winter, and the weight of a tub full of moist soil will be a consideration in the choice both of

Simply shaped specimen topiary in terracotta pots gives Mediterranean detail to the Italianate garden at Vizcaya, Florida.

material and size. Where specimens will occupy permanent sites, on the other hand, the containers must be long lasting and weatherproof.

These criteria effectively exclude plastic materials which, although lightweight, portable and comparatively water-retentive, offer poor insulation against frost; many of these also tend to become discoloured or brittle with age. Concrete and reconstituted stone containers are very heavy to move, which can however be a virtue if it confers stability on taller plants. They sometimes crumble, crack or flake after severe frost, and cheaper versions often look unattractive until weathered over several seasons. However, for permanent sites well-made examples make strong and durable containers.

Timber is traditional, especially formal square boxes constructed so that one side can be removed for repotting. Though expensive to buy they can be made at home from a durable hardwood. Hooped half-barrels are much cheaper and just as compatible with topiary whether they are painted or left natural. They provide good insulation against extreme temperatures and can last for many years as long as the wood

Potted topiary can be positioned to give immediate interest to a view. Here a pair of clipped box bushes are placed to echo the topiary flanking the doorway beyond.

is never allowed to dry completely — this loosens the staves — and the metal hoops are protected from rust.

Although costly, terracotta pots are classic garden features in their own right, especially when decorated with mouldings or impressed designs, and will complement choice pieces of topiary. Their quality varies, however, and some quickly flake or crack after frost. While they share the virtue of clay flower pots in allowing the soil to breathe, like flower pots they tend to dry quickly in hot weather and benefit from being sprayed over when plants are watered. Try to find a range that is explicitly frost-proof, or buy second-hand examples that have proved themselves weather-resistant. The same considerations apply to clay flower pots for restricted specimens, although if they are cracked by frost or manhandling replacement is usually easier and less expensive. The smallest size pot for healthy growth and efficient management is 30cm (12in) in diameter.

Should any clay container start to crack, total breakage can be prevented by neatly 'stitching' the crack at strategic points. Using a fine masonry bit, drill a hole in the rim on each side of the crack, another pair where the crack ends, and more in between if the fracture is a long one. Loop a piece of wire through each pair of holes and twist the ends together tightly on the inside of the pot.

(It is of course vital to check before purchasing that all containers have sufficient drainage holes in the base.)

Planting Containers

Since plants grown in containers are very vulnerable to extreme weather conditions such as frost, drought or waterlogging from prolonged rain, a short period of neglect can cause more damage than to plants in the open ground. More than anywhere else the answer lies in the soil, for a good compost will act as a buffer against these hazards. Peat-based composts are not sufficiently stable for potted trees and shrubs since they can become too wet or dry out to the point where re-wetting is difficult. It is better to include a large proportion of soil to give the compost some resistance to these extremes.

Garden soil is seldom suitable on its own, although it can often be used as a substantial ingredient in the final mixture. Ideally this will combine efficient drainage with enough moisture retention to make frequent watering unnecessary. Where garden soil is in good heart add to every two parts by volume one part each of peat and sharp sand, and mix thoroughly.

Potted trees and topiary are formally arranged on the terraces of the Orangerie at Versailles.

Naturally sandy soils can simply be mixed with an equal volume of peat. If leaf-mould is available this will be better than peat.

Where garden soil is not usable, it is best to buy a good quality prepared soil mix for general use such as, in the UK, an approved John Innes No. 3 potting compost. Do explore the possibility of saving money by buying a loose load if large quantities are needed. Where trees or shrubs are to be confined in small pots, the quality of the planting material is even more critical, and a proprietory mix should always be used in preference to garden soil. If this mixture can be reinforced with a little rotted manure and fibrous loam from turf lifted and left to decay for a season, all the better.

Plant large containers in position; afterwards they will be very heavy to move. Make sure those made of pottery or wood have been soaked first to prevent their absorbing moisture from the prepared compost. Stand the containers on bricks or battens, or place them on ground which will permit surplus water to drain freely away. Cover the bottom of barrels and large tubs and pots with a layer of material such as stones, roughly crushed bricks or broken clay pots — to prevent loss of compost as well as assist drainage. Over this spread a 5cm (2in) layer of moist peat to act as a small water reservoir. Smaller, plastic containers need only the preliminary layer of peat. Fill the container halfway with compost and, using fingertips or the handle of a trowel, firm it evenly, especially around the edges where it tends to be loosest.

Add more compost until it reaches just below the rim, and again firm into place. If a tall standard tree is to be the central feature of the container it will probably need support for the first season or two until securely rooted. Position the plant and drive in a stake close to, but without disturbing, the root ball. Plant against the stake,

setting the tree at or slightly below the previous soil level. Any surrounding plants can then be added. Loosen and level the finished surface, leaving it 5–7cm (2–3in) below the rim on larger pots (30cm/12in or more deep) to allow room for watering. Finally, soak the container until water trickles from its base.

When planting in small pots, pay particular attention to making the compost very firm. It is best to fill the upper half of the pot with the plant in place, trickling the compost around the roots and shaking the pot to settle it. When the pot is filled to 5cm (2in) of the rim, ram the compost down with a trowel handle, and then loosen the surface to allow water to penetrate. Fill to the brim with water and leave to drain.

PLANTING ON BANKS

Sloping ground presents particular problems, apart from the obvious extra care needed (but surprisingly often forgotten) in this situation to make sure new plants are indeed upright. Because rainfall tends to run to waste down a bank rather than soak in, topsoil and mulching materials, together with valuable nutrients, can be washed away from cultivated ground. Precautions have to be taken, therefore, to prevent rapid surface drainage.

Where a new hedge is to be planted across the face of a bank, prepare the ground as usual and then rake the loosened soil to form a level terrace extending the full length of the hedge and at least its proposed width, preferably a little more

Hedges running down banks require special ground preparation. With care, even unconventional subjects such as evergreen azaleas can make a fine formal hedge.

at each side. Tread the terrace firm, rake it level, and it will then be ready for planting. For specimen bushes or for a hedge running up a slope, each plant will need its own prepared site, either levelled or, better still, slightly concave to retain water. Be prepared to water in dry weather more often than on level ground.

PLANTING AGAINST WALLS

The ground close to a wall is often the driest and sometimes the hungriest part of the garden. The area may be sheltered from rainfall, and in summer can dry out rapidly if the wall absorbs moisture from the soil. Measures to protect roots from drought are therefore very important. When preparing the ground remove any rubble and debris left buried after construction. Cultivate a large area because plants are best positioned 30cm (1ft) or so away from the wall rather than immediately beside it, where the dryness would force the roots to search further afield for water. To help retain moisture mix in as much humus — such as peat or garden compost — as possible. Plant normally, leaning the shrub towards the wall, and water the whole area thoroughly. Covering the area with a mulch will delay drying out. If the plant is large enough to secure to the wall, arrange it with its future trained shape in mind.

Support for Wall Shrubs

There are many ways to support shrubs for training on walls, but not all are to be recommended. Although it is relatively easy to hammer wall sprigs or lead-headed nails into a mortar joint wherever needed, many old walls with pitted surfaces and broken or rusting nails testify to the impermanence of this method. To avoid constant renovation later, provide strong and durable support from the start.

It is a waste of time to train shrubs against crumbling or unstable walls; not only are fastenings likely to be insecure, but there is the risk of damaging plants if the wall later needs repair. Unless trellis or wires can be attached to poles erected independently in front of a wall, mortar joints will need to be firm enough to plug for fastenings. Either drill holes and fit wall plugs, or chisel out a short section of the joint and drive in a piece of wide timber lath.

Wooden trelliswork can be screwed or nailed directly into these plugs. A trellis can be made quite simply using widely spaced timber battens, which is not only much cheaper than buying it ready made, but also allows you to

Ivy can be trained on a supporting framework or directly on to a wall, as here where an established plant has been carved into a simple picture.

design the shape of the framework to be hidden eventually behind the mature shrub. Make sure all timber is treated with a suitable wood preservative, used carefully according to the manufacturer's instructions.

Horizontal or vertical wires are much less conspicuous than trellis, although not so immediately decorative. They will need to be threaded about every 2m (6ft) through vine eyes screwed into the plugs or through the holes in the ends of specially designed wall trainers (long, slim wedges of steel hammered home into the plugs). Use galvanized or plastic wire, 10 or 12 gauge, hung 7–10cm (3–4in) away from the wall and arranged so that each main shoot of the plant can be secured as it grows to a parallel wire. After many years the wires will rust away, but by then the plant's branches will be sturdy enough simply to be tied to the surviving wall trainers or vine eyes.

There is no need to provide permanent support for a climber such as ivy that will naturally cling to a wall. When planting this, lay the main shoot horizontally where it can root along its length at the base of the wall and produce a series of vertical side shoots. As these grow, train them to cover a large area quickly by securing them temporarily with self-adhesive plant fasteners.

PRUNING AND TRAINING

PRUNING: AN EXPLANATION

Since the successful management of hedges and topiary depends largely on efficient pruning, it is helpful to understand what happens when the growth of a plant is interrupted, and how this response can be controlled in order to mould the plant into a given shape.

The regular clipping of hedges is not merely a way of suppressing unwanted growth but a method of positively encouraging or guiding a plant's energies. Left unsupervised, a plant will grow in all directions, though primarily upwards until it reaches its maximum sustainable size. It might be assumed that this is a virtue and that plants can therefore be left to mature before they are clipped to shape. However this is not so in practice.

The hormones that control a plant's growth are concentrated mainly around the buds at the apex of shoots, especially those growing vertically or nearly so. Provided its terminal buds are intact, growth will be most pronounced in those regions. Since the plant's energy is necessarily finite, growth will tend to be inhibited elsewhere, with the result that an unpruned shrub often becomes open and thin or excessively congested with vertical shoots, the main branches continuing to extend at the expense of lower ones, which will mark time or even die in the shade cast by unrestrained top growth. If, however, a terminal bud is cut off, energy is redirected into one or two of the dormant buds immediately behind it and these will become dominant instead, each growing to produce a side shoot from the main stem.

Cutting back hedging after planting encourages lateral growth, or bushiness, before the main stems can get too tall. Although some species have a generous supply of lateral buds that can be encouraged to grow, on others these are few or widely spaced. Large-needled conifers are typical of plants whose energies are not so easily re-routed into side shoots, and their reluctance to bush out makes them unsuitable for clipping. This book is concerned with species that quickly respond to pruning by putting out vigorous side shoots, a characteristic that makes them comparatively easy to shape.

Whenever pruning or clipping any plant, therefore, bear in mind that the point is not primarily to control size, though this is obviously an important reason for clipping established hedges and topiary. Remember, too, that the plants will respond in a certain way to pruning. Because clipping removes growing tips and induces lateral growth, this can be a means of persuading healthy plants to bush out and maintain a dense face of foliage. Pruning a branch back to a live bud will stimulate it into growth in whichever direction it is pointing. In this way it is possible to shape the framework of branches in young topiary or precisely control the extension of wall-trained plants.

There is an intimate relationship between top growth and roots, whatever occurs at one end of the plant affecting the other accordingly. For this reason, open-ground stock, whose roots will have been cut when they were lifted from the ground, should have their foliage trimmed correspondingly after planting. On the other hand, the imbalance created by pruning healthy plants normally results in a vigorous flush of new shoots to restore the equilibrium between top and roots. Severe pruning usually provokes a thicket of growth, but partial death of roots may also result if top growth is persistently cut too hard back. Prune or clip regularly, therefore, avoiding the need to cut plants hard. Coax rather than savage plants; they are more responsive than might at first be thought.

A fox is pursued by hounds along the top of a formal yew hedge at Knightshayes Court, Devon.

GOLDEN RULES OF PRUNING

- Never cut without good reason

- Prune at the right time for the species concerned (see *Plant Reference Section* pp. 106–122)

- Never prune in frosty weather, lest shoots die back

- Prune too little rather than too much — more can always be cut off later

- Never prune with blunt tools

PRUNING TOOLS

Careful selection and maintenance of pruning equipment is fundamental to good clipping. Blunt or unsuitable tools leave a ragged finish that is not only visually unsatisfactory but can invite disease. When buying tools, therefore, take some time to test their weight, and choose the best quality you can afford.

Secateurs (Hand Pruners)

There are two basic designs of these single-handed pruning shears. Anvil models have one cutting blade that closes against the face of the opposing blade, or anvil. These tend to be cheaper to buy, but they need very careful use and maintenance to avoid twisting the cutting blade off-centre, and there is always a risk of crushing stems, especially after the blade has lost its keen edge.

By-pass secateurs (hand pruners) are like scissors, the blades crossing one another as they cut. Most have only one sharp edge that operates in the same way as a paper guillotine, although parrot-bill models for light pruning usually cut with both blades. By-pass designs are more comfortable to use, particularly on thicker wood, and tend to leave a cleaner finish.

Insist on handling the tools before buying. There is a wide range of weights and shapes. A few more expensive designs incorporate a handle that revolves as you cut, to reduce the effort involved in prolonged pruning, but this is an unnecessary sophistication for normal garden work. Small pocket models are intended only for occasional trimming and are too lightweight for more intensive topiary use; on the other hand inexperienced gardeners might find heavy-duty kinds tiring. It is worth paying a little extra for a comfortable pair with widely opening blades and slim handles that give efficient leverage. Left-handed models are available, and some manufacturers offer free servicing, replacement blades or long guarantees.

Keep the working parts of secateurs (hand pruners) lightly oiled and free from accumulated sap or plant fibres. Unless they are in constant use, a thorough annual sharpening will be enough, provided the cutting edges are kept keen during the season by occasionally rubbing them up with an oilstone. Tighten the centre nut if there is any play between the blades and test that they will cut through thin paper along their full length without tearing.

Loppers

These are strong, two-handed by-pass pruners with long handles giving the additional leverage necessary to cut through old or thick wood.

Hedging Shears

Long-bladed hedging shears will be needed to trim hedges or small-leafed topiary cleanly to shape, although they are too clumsy for defining great detail. There is little difference between models with straight and serpentine-edged blades, provided they cut cleanly and their handles close against a rubber stop to prevent jarring. Some have a useful notch for cutting through thin, woody stems. Weight, balance and the angle of the handles are all important for comfortable use. Their sharpening and maintenance are the same as for secateurs (hand pruners).

One-Handed Shears (Grass Shears)

These are like miniature hedging shears but operated with one hand, useful in topiary for trimming delicate details.

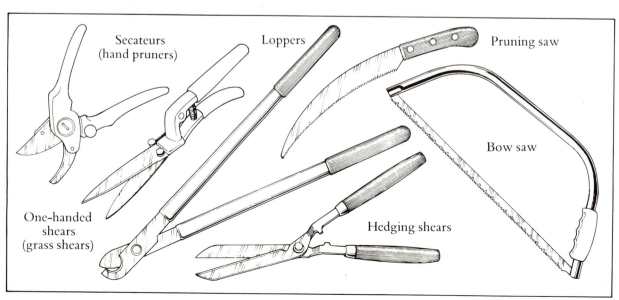

Secateurs (hand pruners)   Loppers   Pruning saw

One-handed shears (grass shears)   Hedging shears   Bow saw

Techniques of formal and informal clipping are combined in this hedge. While the base is shaped conventionally using guide lines, the same plants are clipped freehand above to form the undulating superstructure.

Saws

Two kinds are enough for normal pruning needs. The most useful is the Grecian or pruning saw, which has a narrow, curved blade with teeth set to cut on the pulling stroke; it is invaluable for removing branches in a confined space. A bow or bushman's saw, with a replaceable blade tensioned between the ends of a bent tubular frame, is used for cutting more substantial branches.

Both types are equipped with widely set teeth to cope with green, sappy wood that would clog conventional saws. Grecian saws are sharpened with a triangular file and a saw set, or can be sent away for resharpening. The teeth of bow-saw blades are hardened and cannot be sharpened efficiently. However, their life can often be prolonged by resetting the teeth with a saw set or very carefully with a pair of pliers. They are sharpened to cut in both directions but usually become blunt on the forward edges first; it is often worthwhile to turn the blade round to cut the opposite way.

Keep the blades of saws shiny and free from rust by wiping them after use with an oily cloth.

Electric Hedge-Trimmers

Where a lot of clipping is necessary it is worth investing in a pair of electric hedge-trimmers. Many gardeners prefer these for the comparative ease with which they can be used to maintain the clean faces and precise lines of formal hedging. Both battery-driven and mains-powered models are available; with the latter, always use a residual current device as a safety precaution against serious injury from a cut cable.

HEDGE CLIPPING

To prevent this job from becoming a dreary chore, choose a pleasant day after the last spring frosts, allow plenty of time so that the finish is not spoilt by haste, and make sure your tools are sharp: the work will certainly not be enjoyable if they are blunt and uncomfortable to use. Ornamental hedge trimming is a craft worth taking a pride in, so begin by carefully setting up accurate guide lines.

Drive a stake vertically into the ground beside the hedge at each end and mark on one the level to which you propose to cut. Mark the other stake at the same height from the ground, and tie a garden line between the two points. If a perfectly level top is required on a long hedge, it will be necessary to secure the line to intermediate stakes, wherever it touches each stake when pulled taut. If following the contours of uneven ground, on the other hand, fasten the line to each stake at a consistently measured height. If you are unable to maintain the level across the width of the hedge by eye, erect a similar guide

To cut an accurate batter an adjustable jig was traditionally used. This photograph shows a typical frame used by a gardener at Great Dixter, Sussex, early this century.

gardeners used a simple jig, easily made and adjustable to measure different degrees of batter (see illustration).

One can readily be constructed from planed softwood, using 7.5 x 7.5cm (3 x 3in) timber for the upright and the diagonal arm (each around 2m/6ft long), and 5 x 2.5cm (2 x 1in) timber for the adjustable cross-bar or stay, which should be 60cm (2ft) long. Join the upright and arm at the base with a strong hinge. Drill a series of holes centrally at 5cm (2in) intervals along one half of the stay, and screw the other end to the top of the arm, loosely so that it can still be moved. Fix a stout nail or peg near the top of the upright to hold the stay at the required extension. Finally, suspend a weighted string from the top of the upright as a plumb line to check it is vertical when used.

Alternatively, join at one end two pieces of timber, long enough to rest their free ends on the ground on both sides of the hedge, straddling it at the angle to which it is to be cut. Nail a cross-piece between the two legs at the finished level of the top of the hedge, so producing an 'A' frame whose lower outline matches the proposed cross-section of the hedge. Stand the frame against each end of the hedge in turn, and mark the width of the top on each side with additional guide lines. Roughly trim the shoulders of the hedge to these. Then, starting from one end and using the frame repeatedly to check the angle, carefully clip an evenly sloping face on each side.

When both sides have been clipped, clear away all the trimmings. The next few trims can often be done without guide lines, clipping back to the levels established earlier, until once again the hedge needs shaping. As long as the batter remains clear, it will be unnecessary to use the jig or 'A' frame. Instead, use a length of string as a simple guide for clipping the sides, stretching it taut between the top guide line (positioned at the intended finished level of the face) and a second line at the base of the hedge. Knot this vertical string loosely so that you can slide it along the face as a guide while cutting. Trim the top and ends of the face first; if you stand sideways on to the hedge while working, you will find it is relatively easy to sight along the shears and clip a level face the first time.

Cutting to a guide line is particularly important for low hedges, since it is difficult to judge heights and levels when looking down from above. When working on tall hedges, it will be necessary to arrange a plank of wood securely fastened between stable trestles or steps so that you can cut from a comfortable height.

line along the other top edge, and tie a third line between the two, loosely knotted so that you can slide it along.

Always clip the top of a hedge first, beginning by cutting along the shoulder to establish the level set by the guide line. If the hedge is more than 60cm (2ft) wide, cut from one side to half its width and then finish from the other side, otherwise the weight of the shears may cause you unwittingly to cut downwards into the hedge as you work away from yourself. Use the hedging shears whichever way up proves more comfortable, although you will probably find that with the handles tilted downwards it is easier to judge the top level by eye. Lightly sweep the clippings to the ground as you progress to avoid their covering uncut growth, taking care not to disturb the lie of the growth so that you have to trim the top again.

With the top complete, you can begin to clip the sides. Usually these will be cut to a more or less oblique angle, or batter, so that the hedge is narrower at the top and light can easily reach all the foliage. To shape the batter for the first time, a wooden template will be needed. Traditionally,

SPECIAL HEDGES

Plashed Hedges

Though plashed or 'laid' hedges — deciduous hedges with branches woven like basketwork — are only seen today in agricultural use, they can look highly decorative, and have in the past been used ornamentally in the garden.

A hedge to be trained in this way must be taller than the intended finished level, because it should already have strong and regularly spaced main stems that can be bent down and interwoven between others left upright for support.

The work is done in winter when the framework of stems is visible and accessible. First clear any weeds and debris from the hedge, and then thin the branches to a series of vertical stems. Choose particularly strong stems about

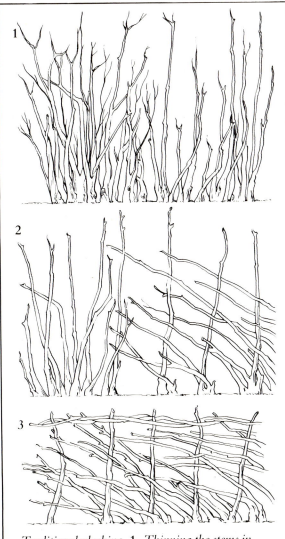

Traditional plashing. **1.** *Thinning the stems in winter.* **2.** *Stems being interwoven between evenly spaced uprights.* **3.** *The finished hedge cut to height with tops braided.*

30–45cm (12–18in) apart to form the uprights, and trim these down to the height of the finished hedge, making sure that there is one at each end; where there are no suitably straight stems, insert strong stakes as uprights instead. The intervening stems are then cut part-way through near their base so they can be bent, all in the same direction, and woven one above the next between the uprights. When a hedge is trained professionally, stems are cut with downward strokes of a billhook — a heavy, broad-bladed chopper with a hooked tip. A saw is just as effective, if the stems are cut between half and two-thirds of the way through and then bent back, away from the cut.

Traditionally, the tops of the plashed stems are secured by braiding flexible hazel rods or brambles around them. An alternative is to braid them with two lengths of wire, fastened to the end posts and to some of the uprights along the hedge. After braiding the stems, trim them to define the top and ends of the hedge.

The resulting framework will support a slender hedge which should be trimmed during the growing season and clipped hard back each winter to the original weave.

Pollarding

This decorative technique is practised on deciduous trees which have reached or exceeded the desired height — usually about 2.5–3m (8–9ft). When starting with young stocks, allow them to grow upwards unchecked. If the intention is only to pollard the top, trim any lower feathers cleanly off at the trunk to leave just the topmost branches each year; rub off any buds that break later around the cuts.

Let the trees grow for a season beyond the required height and then, after the leaves have fallen, prune the leading shoots back to this level. Cut off any branches remaining at the top altogether or shorten them back to about 60cm (2ft) long. In future years, cut all new growth back to these points in winter, leaving a neatly rounded finish to the ends, which will develop over the seasons into swollen knobs.

Prune trees to be formed into a pollarded tunnel in the same way, but leave the topmost side shoots growing until they can be bent over the intervening path and tied temporarily, either to each other or to arched metal formers. Trim off any unwanted shoots. Those you are training over the tunnel can be stopped wherever you want a head of growth at which to prune; space these points evenly so that the tunnel is covered by a thick canopy in summer but presents a regular pattern of bare branches in winter.

To form a narrow pollarded screen or hedge, leave regularly placed branches to grow horizontally along the line of the hedge. Train branches from adjacent trees towards each other along parallel horizontal wires and stop them where they meet. As side shoots appear on these branches, thin them to regular distances, rubbing off surplus shoots and leaving those that remain to grow for a season. At the end of the year, prune them back almost to their base. Maintain this lateral pollarding annually.

When you have completed the framework of pollarded shoots, remove all ties and formers.

Pleaching

This is almost a combination of pollarding and laying, since the height of pleached trees is kept restricted while their flexible side growth is

Opposite: pollarded trees still present stark outlines in spring; leafy growth will not appear for some weeks.
Below: a hornbeam tunnel. The closely planted main stems are trained over a firm framework while the branches are pleached to form the walls. Lateral growth may need thinning as well as clipping as trees mature.

trained or interwoven as it grows to form a dense, narrow hedge. Either erect a series of wires 60cm (2ft) apart and stretched between vertical poles or, if the young trees are close enough to each other, tie canes between their trunks to which the branches can be secured.

Tie in those shoots that grow horizontally along the hedge; these will form its woven or trained framework. Shoots which grow out from the face of this framework are pruned in the same way as the sides of a conventional hedge. If you are making a stilt hedge where the top portion is pleached above the bare trunks of the trees, either remove the feathers as the trees grow or prune away the lower branches from existing trees to leave the stems clean and the underside of the raised hedge level.

Once the pleached hedge is formed the supporting wires and poles can be removed, or left in place if they are not conspicuous.

Fruit Hedges

An existing row of gooseberry bushes can easily be transformed into a fruitful and impenetrable hedge if the plants are close enough together and

Tall stilt hedges of pleached hornbeam make a curving colonnade at Dumbarton Oaks in Washington D.C.

branch from near ground level; gaps lower down between bushes grown on legs might prove difficult to fill in. Where bushes are more than 1m (1yd) apart, layer one or two of the bottom branches in the space (see p.53).

Planting prepared cuttings directly into place is the easiest way to start a gooseberry hedge, especially if their rooting is hastened by mulching the ground first with black plastic (see p. 59). Take the cuttings in the autumn, cutting pieces around 30cm (1ft) long from the end of the current season's shoots. Instead of stripping the lower buds, normally done to produce a clean leg for easy maintenance, merely remove the growing tip and leave the rest of the buds intact; the hedge will need the resulting basal growth if it is to be clothed right to the ground.

Plant the cuttings in pairs, pushing them to half their length into the ground 30cm (1ft) apart, slanting each pair at an angle of 45 degrees so that they lean towards the next pair down the row. If using a black plastic mulch, cut a cross at each station and plant through the crosses. Shorten new growth by half every autumn until the hedge is formed, and then clip it to shape with shears two or three times a year, delaying the first cut of the season until immediately after any fruit has been gathered.

Red and white currants can be treated similarly. The myrobalan or cherry plum (*Prunus cerasifera*) also makes an attractive fruit hedge; it grows true from seed or can be raised from hard-wood cuttings. To avoid gaps in the hedge from failure to root or germinate, start the plants in a nursery bed and transfer them later, when you can identify the strongest. Plant and clip in the same way as gooseberries.

CLIPPING TOPIARY

Although the mechanics of clipping topiary are very similar to cutting a hedge, there are significant differences, the most important being the greater attention that must be paid to overall symmetry. This quality or its absence is much more obvious at a glance than it might be with a hedge, which is usually seen only from one side.

Geometrical topiary with flat faces and squared edges is possibly the hardest of all to keep balanced and visually satisfying, and the care required should never be underestimated. Unless you have a good eye and a practised hand, you will probably need to guide your cutting with lines, wooden jigs and even a level. Use a plumb line for the perpendicular faces of specimens, and a level on a board resting between two stakes to check that the tops are straight where accuracy seems critical. Only

Clipped balls of yew grouped on a sloping lawn at Keir House in Dunblane, Scotland. A balanced shape, and dense and healthy growth are more important than cutting a perfect sphere.

trust your skill unaided where the outline has been carefully cut already the same season, or where restricted views of the topiary make precision unnecessary. Adjusting a mistake or over-enthusiastic cutting on one face may entail clipping that entire side again, and also the opposite face to maintain the balance.

Contrary to first impresssions, rounded topiary is easier to clip well. The major difficulty with spherical shapes is that little practical help can be given by guides and lines, although where topiary has been trained around wire formers these may still be distinguishable beneath the foliage and used as guides.

Generally the work must be done freehand, starting in the middle of any curve to establish the finished surface; then, using this as a reference point, continue round the curve in both directions. With a sphere, first trim the top and cut downwards from this on two sides to trim a ring whose symmetry you can assess from where you stand. Then clip another ring at 90 degrees to the first, leaving four distinct quarters of the ball to trim clean. Go carefully to avoid removing more foliage than you can spare.

At Great Dixter, animated squirrels have been trained above strictly clipped geometrical blocks of yew. Few plants are as versatile as yew for both clipping and training.

Electric hedge-trimmers are easier to handle for shaping smoothly curved surfaces, though less adaptable for clipping figures than hedging shears, whose points are valuable for cleaning out corners and crevices. Always trim with the ends of the blades of hedging shears; using their full length risks cutting flat faces on a sphere.

Free-form topiary offers greater latitude than geometrical shapes for the correction of superficial mistakes in clipping, but a serious error here might mean the loss of a feature and require lengthy retraining. Even with the simplest figures, it is still advisable to work from the top downwards and from the centre outwards, cutting both sides together to keep them balanced. If you trim a whole side first, it could be difficult to cut the other exactly the same, and you might find yourself shaving a little more from each alternately in the attempt to match them. Do not try to manipulate hedging shears around fine detail; they are too clumsy for this, and it is easier to use either secateurs (hand pruners) or single-handed trimmers.

Although it is feasible to carve complex free topiary from hitherto unrestricted trees, always remember that beneath the foliage is an established network of branches that might get in the way. On mature trees these branches may be long and substantial, making it difficult to carve great detail or cut deep into the foliage without encountering a main branch. Severing this could also remove a large section of foliage from the upper part of the tree.

If a branch does obstruct the shape, check first how much growth it supports and whether you can really afford to sacrifice it all. If not, there is little choice but to modify the design to include it. This will probably mean simplifying the plan or abandoning a detail, but the only alternative would be to prune the whole tree hard back and start developing the shape from the resulting new growth.

It is much easier to shape mature trees into simple solid bodies as this usually involves cutting only the outer foliage and younger wood back to the new surface, without major surgery on the structure of the tree. Prune the tree back in the same way as for an overgrown hedge (see pp. 100–101), cutting within the eventual form and reserving a fine finish, together with any incidental detail, until the branches are covered once more with a layer of young growth, when you can start sculpting and clipping the tree to its final shape.

TRAINING PRINCIPLES

Training is complementary, not an alternative, to redirecting growth by pruning or clipping. If you are creating figurative topiary or a design on a wall, for example, you can first produce a shoot just where you need it by cutting back to a suitably placed bud, but once grown it must be trained to fit the proposed shape.

Only the simplest aids are required for training: string — preferably tarred (weatherproofed) because it lasts longer but eventually decays, unlike plastic twine which must be cut away once redundant if it is not to choke shoots as they mature; wire — either flexible and covered in plastic, or the thin kind used by florists; clothes pegs; garden canes; and sometimes a training frame made from heavy-duty fencing wire, metal or wooden laths.

Much can be achieved simply by tying young shoots either together or to a guide frame. For example, the quickest way to start creating a sitting bird or a ball on the top of a hedge is to leave several strong adjacent shoots unclipped and tie them together in a bundle. As these grow they can be spread out and tied to a wire form; unwanted side shoots can be pruned out and others retained to fill in the body of the shape.

Below: hunting scene at Ladew Topiary Gardens, Maryland; such complex topiary forms are usually trained over a wire frame. Right: stages in training of the topiary hounds at Knightshayes Court.

Make sure the ties are secure but not so tight that there is no room for the shoot to swell as it grows. Never try to change the direction of an older, more rigid branch too dramatically. Green shoots are pliable enough to be bent without damage, but woodier ones are liable to crack unless trained in stages. Bend an older branch part of the way towards its new position and secure it with a long piece of string. When it shows no sign of springing back if released, shorten the tie to bend it a little further. Repeat this cautiously until the branch is in position.

Branches trained on wires or trellis against walls must similarly be tied in while young, or moved in stages. If it is difficult to keep one straight while you progressively lower it, tie a garden cane to the supports and secure the branch to this at several points, lowering cane and branch together each time until you can tie the branch to a wire and remove the cane.

Where a shoot is to be trained outwards, to fill a hole or to form a projection from a topiary figure for example, it must be secured firmly in some way, perhaps to another branch nearby. Failing this, tie one end of the string to a point about half-way along the shoot and the other end to the base of the main stem. If the plant has a stake, it may be possible to nail a piece of lath to this horizontally as an armature; tie the shoot in to this and swivel the armature to the required position in stages as the shoot develops.

Sometimes it will be impossible to tie a shoot down in any of these ways. Instead, the free end of the string can be fixed to a peg or cane hammered into the ground some distance from the plant, or to a suitable weight. Alternatively, wire the shoot by twisting thin but resilient wire in a gentle spiral around its stem from end to end; the wired shoot should then stay in place wherever it is bent. Even clothes pegs can be useful: one clamped around a main stem close above a young side shoot to be trained outwards will force the shoot down so that it grows out at the required angle.

It can be observed that training a shoot down from the perpendicular alters its rate of growth: the lower the shoot is bent, the slower its extension. If it is bent in an arc, sap tends to flow freely up as far as the highest point, where the buds will be the quickest to break into growth, and is then checked as it turns downwards so that the lowest buds grow slowly, if at all. This phenomenon can be exploited as a further method of regulating growth, but it does mean that you should not bend branches too far downwards at an early stage if you want side shoots to grow uniformly along their length.

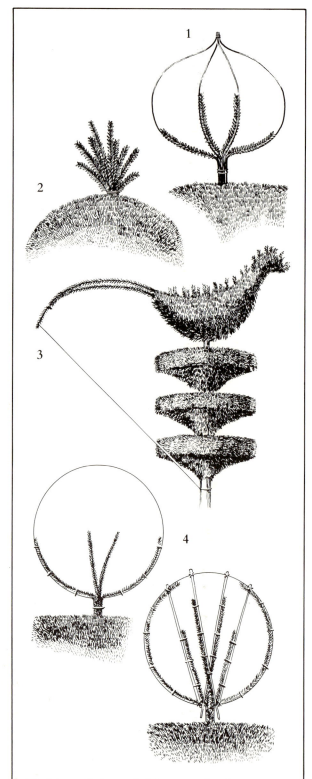

Training techniques. **1.** *Training a finial on a wire frame.* **2.** *Growing shoots tied into a bundle: the foundation for any shape on top of a hedge.*
3. *Changing the direction of a shoot by tying down.*
4. *Two stages of filling in a solid shape by fanning out the young stems and tying them to canes attached across the frame.*

Dedicated trainers of fruit manipulate growth by close attention to individual buds, rubbing off those in the wrong place, or pinching out a terminal bud to stimulate those lower down. Similarly, when training detailed topiary, a lot of pruning can be avoided by selecting buds or shoots while still young and pinching or rubbing off others before they need cutting away. Inactive buds can be induced to grow by cutting a shallow notch in the stem immediately above, which impedes the flow of sap and diverts it sideways into the bud. A nick close below a bud, on the other hand, will usually prevent its growing, while keeping it still alive for possible revival later by notching above.

TRAINING TOPIARY

Whereas carved topiary can often begin to look respectable a year after you first shape it from a naturally grown tree, with trained specimens you may have to wait three or four years, sometimes more, before the initial framework begins to fill into a solid body — the period dictated by the rate of growth of the particular plant. For very detailed topiary, this plant will almost inevitably be yew. Although other plants with long flexible growth can be trained into simple formal shapes, only yew is sufficiently malleable to tolerate training into delicate or complex topiary forms.

With these limitations in mind, examine an established tree you would like to train. First stand back and view it from all angles to assess its potential. Often its natural shape will suggest an appropriate design. Then explore the framework of branches to check that the principal shoots required for the design are in approximately the right places; surplus branches can always be removed but it takes time to grow an additional shoot to take its place in the framework. Having modified or confirmed the tentative design, you can start to train the tree.

Younger specimens planted deliberately for training can usually be shaped at an early stage from ground level, perhaps by supporting the main design on a clipped plinth of foliage — especially where several trees have been planted together for rapid effect — or by pruning away side shoots to reveal a clean stem. Where two or more plants are intended to form the 'legs' of a design, their lower side shoots can be trimmed but not pruned completely, so that they seem an integral part of the clipped figure rather than bare supports.

Select the stems that will form the main ribs of the design, either a single shoot or several tied in a bundle, leaving their ends free for training above this constriction. Bunching several together is helpful if you intend to spread out side shoots from this main rib, for example when forming a solid shape on top of a hedge; it will also save time where density is important. Cut out all redundant stems, leaving those needed for training.

At this point some kind of frame will be needed. This is best made from thick fencing wire, which has the resilience to hold a symmetrical curve when bent and soon becomes invisible beneath the foliage; wood is too clumsy and perishable for use except as timber 'scaffolding' to support complex shapes. Bend the wire to form a rudimentary template to which shoots can be tied as they grow. Leave enough wire free to attach the frame to the main stem of the tree, or to a supporting cane, or for pegging into the soil when specimens are to be trained from ground level.

Always use the minimum amount of wire practicable, where possible exploiting the natural elasticity of a shoot instead of tying it, which in excess can deaden some designs. For example, it makes little difference whether the stiff handles of a topiary urn are made from shoots trained up a pair of wire formers or by tying two long stems downwards into place. On the other hand, the tail of a topiary bird or animal will seem much more life-like if it has been strained into place by bending the stem down with a length of string.

Where a wire shape is used to define an outline, tie the stems to it with string until they meet around its perimeter, trimming any side shoots that form and pinching out the main stems where they join. If the shape is to be filled as a solid body, fan out the stems and train them across it like the ribs of a leaf, using transverse canes for additional support if necessary. Stop the shoots when they reach the far side. Side shoots will eventually fill the intervening spaces and hide the wire with their foliage.

Do not expect the design to develop uniformly. Larger areas naturally take longer to become evenly covered with foliage and quite often the tail of a bird, for example, will still be growing after its head is fully shaped. Growth on the side facing the sun is usually markedly more rapid than that on the opposite side of a bush, even with yew which is comparatively unaffected by shade. Either design the topiary in the first place to take account of greater vigour on the sunny side, or accept that the work will develop unevenly. It is no disgrace to let people see work in progress.

SPECIAL EFFECTS

Ivy Sculpture

Ivy can be carved on a wall into two-dimensional topiary. Because of their relatively large leaves and prolific growth, varieties of ivy normally grown outdoors are best suited to simple patterns and outlines. A small-scale shape could be trained from young plants, while larger designs (such as that on p.67) are more easily and rapidly carved from ivy that is already established on a wall.

Where the plant covers a large expanse, cut through the stems with secateurs (hand pruners) using brick courses or the edges of the wall as guides. Old, tough branches will be fixed firmly to the wall and you may have to lever these away with a chisel or screwdriver before you can cut them. Carefully pull away surplus growth from around the design, using a paint scraper to remove stems at their roots and also to avoid damaging the fabric of the wall.

Small blocks of foliage can be cut from within the outline in the same way. Ivy stems tend to meander up a wall, however, and you will be very lucky not to cut through any that support sections of foliage you want to retain. Where this happens, small areas of the design could die off. Young growth from surrounding stems will soon cover any dead patches, and you can encourage this by twining new shoots amongst the

An almost life-size camel trained in ivy at Longwood Gardens, Pennsylvania. Ivy can be shaped into complex figures over a wire frame.

old stems. Make sure before cutting that you will not sever any of the basal stems and so risk losing much of the established growth.

Once the picture is carved, its edges will need trimming with secateurs (hand pruners) two or three times a year as shoots grow out across the cleared wall. In early spring, it is a good idea to lightly shear off the old foliage on the face of the design to keep it flat against the wall; young leaves will soon appear to cover any bareness.

Ivy is sometimes used to edge topiary grown in pots and containers. The plants should be spaced 15cm (6in) apart around the rim and trained up through wire netting bent in the shape of a narrow tunnel. Foliage will quickly cover this and develop into a low hedge which can be clipped two or three times a year.

Small-leaved ivy and other trailing or climbing plants, such as creeping ficus species, *Stephanotis floribunda* and ornamental vines such as cissus and rhoicissus, are ideal for training into decorative shapes on wires, either in the garden or indoors according to hardiness. Their long, flexible stems can be twined or tied around wire formers, while the tips of shoots are constantly pinched out to encourage bushy growth. The wire frames eventually disappear from view, and the plants will stand the light trimming necessary to maintain a neat finish. No special cultivation is required, but it is essential that the wire formers are firmly fixed from the start, since the climbing plants will always depend on them for support. For this reason, take care with pot-grown specimens to protect the super-structure from disturbance during repotting.

Cloud-pruning can be used to emphasize the flowing habit as well as the attractive woody structure of such species as juniper.

Cloud Pruning

Very little topiary work makes a point of accentuating the stems of plants, which in most cases merely provide support, either invisibly or as an insignificant part of the design. The oriental technique of cloud pruning, however, is deliberately practised on species whose main stems are as interesting as their foliage. Although normally confined to trees growing in the open garden, this kind of pruning can be adapted to specimens trained loosely against a wall.

Trees are pruned to reveal as much as possible of the beauty and form of their stem structure, reducing the foliage to neatly rounded 'clouds' at the ends of branches or distributed down their length. A preliminary design based on the growth pattern of the tree should be made before starting work because mistakes will be very conspicuous. Carve the whole tree as a piece of topiary, cutting away surplus growth to reveal clean stems, and shaping the concentrations of twigs that remain so that each is an independent rounded body of foliage that can be kept clipped in future seasons.

Ornamental Espaliers

Training fruit in decorative and highly productive designs either on walls or along wires has a long pedigree. Espaliering, as this elegant art is known, can also be applied to many flowering shrubs, which can be trained into a variety of ornamental shapes using wire or trellis supports (see p.67). It is important to make sure the species chosen is sufficiently vigorous to cover a given area, and that it will stand the restrictive pruning necessary to maintain the formal lines of the design.

Start with a young shrub that has a strong main stem. Plant this centrally against the wall so that the evolving pattern will not unbalance growth. Tie in the stem vertically and cut it just above the first wire. Several shoots will grow

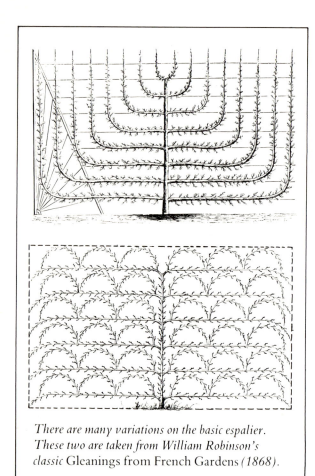

There are many variations on the basic espalier. These two are taken from William Robinson's classic Gleanings from French Gardens *(1868).*

long stems can be tied down in arcs ('festooned') for a rounded pattern, a technique which will also encourage side shoots to develop along the upper surface of the arc. However, try to keep espaliers simple, their branches evenly spaced, otherwise only very frequent pruning will keep the design clearly visible. Once it is established, prune an ornamental espalier according to species, cutting or pinching out all new growing tips to prevent further expansion.

(For species suitable as espaliers, see the *Plant Reference Section* pp. 106-122.)

Inarch Grafting

Conventional topiary can also be combined with the decorative training of stems. Spirals for example can be shaped to reveal the barleysugar twist of the trunk, while an open cake-stand arrangement is enhanced by intervening sections

The stem of a clipped standard, such as this bay, can be ornamented with inarch grafting.

out from this during the following season. Retain and tie in as many as you need for the main ribs of the design: for example, the top two shoots can be trained, one to each side, to provide the horizontal base for a series of vertical shoots. For a conventional espalier tie the topmost shoot vertically, cutting it again above the second wire to repeat the process, and train the second and third shoots sideways. Remove all other shoots entirely, or cut them back to only four or five leaves if short flowering or fruiting spurs are wanted.

For a fan shape, retain as many strong stems as the shrub has produced the first season and spread them out evenly across the face of the wall, tying them to the wires where they cross, or to canes already secured at the required angles. If not enough stems appear after the first season, multiply them by tying in those you have and cutting all or some back to encourage each to produce two or three new stems.

Remember that cutting a stem back to a bud will divert growth in the direction in which the bud is pointing. This, combined with physically restraining stems by tying them to the wires, allows considerable scope for the design of espaliers. They are not restricted to angular patterns:

of clean straight stem. By means of inarch or approach grafting, two pieces of stem can be united to continue their growth as one, a valuable technique if you need to join separate plants at some point, or want to decorate a bare section of stem with a circular, diamond-shaped or triangular 'window'.

To form such a shape, prune the main stem of the tree to produce two side shoots and tie these around a wire frame until they meet. Instead of stopping their growth at that point, tie them together, bend them upwards and allow them to grow on parallel to each other, grafting them together the following spring to become one again. The simplest way to do this is by slicing a strip from each shoot at the point where they meet, to expose a similarly sized area of bare tissue on each. Bind the two cut surfaces together with raffia and seal the union with pruning paint. Leave for a season or two for the join to callus over, when one of the shoots can be cut back to the union.

This kind of grafting occurs naturally where two branches of a tree cross one another, and can be found frequently amongst the stems of ivy on a wall. It has other decorative uses in the garden: for example, the living trellis of a pleached hedge can be reinforced by approach grafting horizontal side shoots from adjacent trees in the manner described.

Budding

Another decorative grafting technique, particularly valuable for ornamenting the tops of hedges, is budding, by which two contrasting varieties of a species can be grafted together. This technique is most commonly seen with holly hedges, but can be applied to other species (see p. 40).

In budding, a leaf bud from a new variety is united with a stem of an existing plant of the same species or a suitable root stock. This is usually done late in the growing season using buds from the current year's growth.

Cut off a section of shoot with several good buds on it, each at the base of a leaf stalk. With a very sharp knife, remove each bud, starting about 1.25cm (½in) below the leaf stalk and cutting into the stem behind the bud to emerge at least 2.5cm (1in) above. Cut off the leaf to leave a piece of stalk just long enough to hold as a handle while fitting the bud in place.

Cut a 'T'-shaped incision through the bark of the stem on which the bud is to be grafted, making the leg of the 'T' the same length as the bud section. Lift the two flaps of cut bark, slide the bud into place and secure it by tying the bark together with raffia. To produce a head of foliage quickly when grafting a new variety on to the hedge, insert three buds on the one stem, evenly spaced around the stem so that the incisions are not concentrated too closely together.

Leave the top growth on the main stem until the buds are actively producing young shoots; often the transferred buds may not grow until the following spring. They can sometimes be encouraged to grow by removing a narrow ring of bark from the stem above the graft, or, if only one bud is grafted, by bending the main stem so that the bud points upwards. Once the grafts are growing, cut the main stem down to the union and start shaping the new growth as if it were the head of a tree.

Budding. **1.** *The shoot before cutting.* **2.** *The prepared bud.* **3.** *'T'-shaped incision in root stock.* **4.** *The bud slipped into place.* **5.** *The bud secured with raffia.*

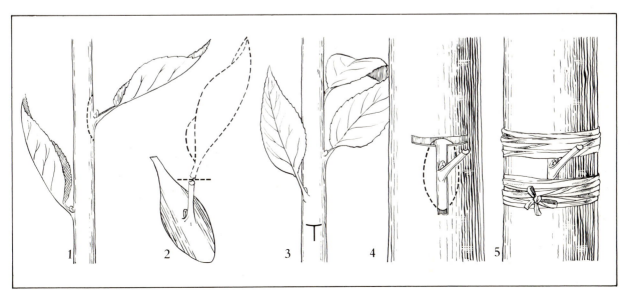

PROJECTS

Obelisk

Although it would be possible to roughly carve an obelisk freehand, for geometric precision it is best to revive a method of shaping topiary that was popular many years ago: using a wire cage as a former around the plant and clipping off the shoots as they protrude. The former is left in place and eventually disappears beneath the surface of the finished work. This method is particularly valuable for architectural forms, especially as an aid to achieving flat, symmetrical faces. The example given here uses privet for rapid development; other plants such as yew or Handsworth box are equally suitable, although the wire former will remain visible for much longer before disappearing behind the foliage.

These directions are for an obelisk a little over 180cm (6ft) high. In this and the examples that follow measurements can of course be varied proportionately according to the plant species used and the size required.

First year
Plant a bushy specimen of *Ligustrum ovalifolium* in prepared ground or cut back an established bush to form a narrow, upright column with a

Development of obelisk. **1.** *Wire panel cut to shape for the former.* **2.** *Newly planted bushy specimen.* **3.** *Dense growth is encouraged by clipping foliage back against the former.* **4.** *Completed obelisk.*

square section less than 60cm (2ft) wide. Around this construct a cage in the shape of an obelisk, using four panels of 5cm (2in) mesh wire netting. Cut each panel 180cm (6ft) high, 60cm (2ft) wide at the base and 45cm (18in) wide at the top. Around the plant push a 240cm (8ft) cane firmly into the ground at each corner and secure the wire panels to these with wire plant rings or thin plastic twine. Make sure the cage looks perfectly upright from all sides, and leave the top open. Clip nearly flush with the netting any growth that protrudes during the first season.

Second year onwards
As the bush develops continue to trim growth that appears through the wire, leaving it a little proud so that the netting is gradually hidden by the superficial foliage. When the bush protrudes beyond the top of the cage, cut it to form a flattened four-sided pyramid to crown the obelisk. After the finished shape has been formed, the wire cage can, if desired, be carefully removed if it is no longer needed as a guide for clipping.

Yew Spiral

Spirals are ideal subjects for freestanding topiary or for small tubs or large pots. This example uses yew but the vigorous Handsworth box could also be trained into this form. A box spiral might be trained as high as 3m (10ft); one in yew could be taller still.

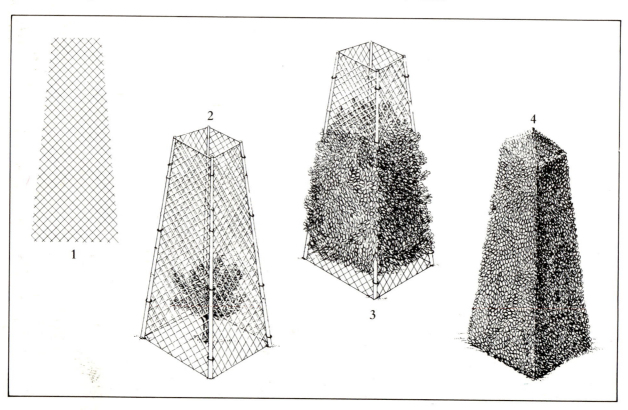

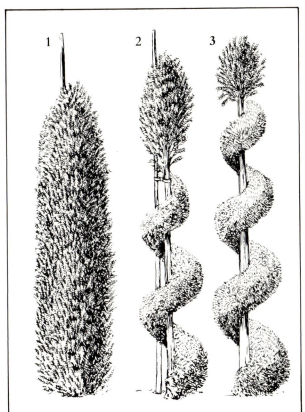

Development of spiral. **1.** *Young tree planted against stake and trained into a cylindrical shape.* **2.** *The first two rings of the spiral.* **3.** *The spiral is developed progressively, tapering towards the top.*

First year

Choose a bushy young yew tree about 45–60cm (18in–2ft) tall with a strong, straight vertical stem. Prepare the ground thoroughly and provide a stake or stout cane about 180cm (6ft) tall for the tree. Plant the yew close beside this and tie the main shoot securely to the cane to keep the leader perfectly vertical. Do not cut back any of the foliage at this stage.

Second year

Continue to tie in the leader as it grows. In early summer after the last frosts prune all the longer side shoots back to about 10cm (4in) long, to leave a straight pillar of foliage to bush out to its final length of about 15cm (6in) or so. If growth is vigorous during the season, lightly clip it back again to the basic cylinder in early autumn.

Third year onwards

Repeat the second year's maintenance. As soon as the tree is about 120cm (4ft) tall, start cutting the foliage to form the lowest full revolution of the spiral. Bear in mind that the lowest revolution will be the longest, since the intervals between spirals will decrease with height: on larger

yew specimens with an eventual height well over 180cm (6ft), the first spiral could be trained to wind full circle about 90cm (3ft) from the ground; on smaller specimens the spirals would of course be much closer. Cut into the foliage with secateurs (hand pruners) at the point where the first revolution will be completed, measuring from the ground, and snip away enough foliage to reveal a small bare area of stem. Repeat this at soil level on the same side, and halfway up on the opposite side. Join these three points in a smooth spiral by cutting out a channel back to the bare stem. The winding band of side shoots that is left might look thin and tufty, but over the years clipping will thicken it into a dense ridge of foliage.

In succeeding years, repeat this process of training and clipping, dispensing with the stake when the tree reaches its full height. Clip the spiral to leave flat faces above and below the ridge of foliage, and a straight finish on the outer edge about 8–20cm (6–8in) away from the main stem.

Many variations are possible on the traditional yew spiral, here set on a rounded plinth and topped with a conical cap.

'Potted' Tree

For this *trompe l'oeil* piece of topiary, both the square pot and the mop-head standard tree are trained plants, in this case green and golden privet. Many other species could be used equally well: choose a dwarf or semi-vigorous hedge plant to form the pot, and for the centrepiece any naturally small tree or one that looks decorative when clipped as a standard, such as sweet bay.

Golden privet (*Ligustrum ovalifolium* 'Aureum') shows its colour to best advantage when kept fairly low by regular clipping, and it is therefore an ideal plant for shaping into the 'pot', which will usually be about 45cm (18in) high. For the standard centrepiece, one of the larger, green forms of privet, such as *L. lucidum*, would be suitable.

For a 'pot' 90cm (3ft) square.

Development of 'potted' tree. **1.** *Dwarf plants set around a young standardized tree.* **2.** *Bushy hedge growth is encouraged by early clipping.* **3.** *The completed 'pot'.*

First year

Thoroughly prepare an area of ground about 120cm (4ft) square.

The tree that will form the centrepiece could be purchased from a nursery as a standard; if, however, you intend to train it yourself, plant the young specimen in the centre of the area, firmly securing the leading shoot to a vertical stake 120–150cm (4–5ft) tall. During the first winter, shorten side shoots to about 5–7cm (2–3in) long.

To plant the 'pot', first mark out a square 75cm (30in) across on the ground around the tree, measuring carefully from its stem, not the stake supporting it. Set out the plants along this outline, positioning one at each corner and filling in the rest of each side with another one or more according to species (for recommended spacing and treatment see relevant entry in *Plant Reference Section* pp.106–122).

Second year onwards

Continue to tie in the leading shoot of the standard. During the second winter, shorten any new side shoots as before and completely cut off the side shoots shortened in the previous year. When the standard reaches a height a little above the centre of the intended head, pinch out the tip and allow the most recently formed side shoots to develop into a framework of branches.

Begin to clip the 'pot' to shape in early summer; even though plants will not have reached their intended size, cutting the shape now will help growth to fill out evenly. Cut the outer face of each side to lean gently outwards, keeping the inner faces vertical and leaving a clear space around the stem of the standard. Either round off the top of each side or cut it square. Aim to shape a pot with an outside measurement of about 90cm (3ft) square, with each side 30cm (1ft) thick.

House Number

Several kinds of plants such as pyracantha or evergreen cotoneaster can be used for espalier training in the shape of a number or name on a house wall (for suitable species, see *Plant Reference Section* pp.106–122).

First year

Decide whereabouts the number is to be displayed and its size: for clarity the figures will probably need to be at least 60cm (2ft) high. Secure a piece of trellis to the wall as a permanent background for the number, or arrange wires which can eventually be removed. Each figure will require a separate plant, which should be set immediately below its centre (see

Development of house number espaliered on wall. Training wires can be removed when the figures are completed, unless still required for support.

in even curves and tying them frequently. Where a shoot must change direction suddenly, cut off the growing tip to force a branch to form at an angle. Any side stems not needed to form the figure should be pinched or trimmed back to about 5cm (2in) to start dressing the stem with foliage. When the figure has been shaped pinch the tip out of the main shoot or shoots and concentrate on clothing the stems with short side shoots. These can be trimmed with shears on straight sections, while curved portions are best clipped with secateurs (hand pruners); use shears to keep the outer face uniform.

Cock Pheasant

As with any topiary bird or animal the shape must be simplified to take account of the natural growth of the medium and the practicalities of keeping the outline cleanly clipped. More important than detail is achieving a characteristic pose that gives life and realism to the finished work. For the pheasant, yew is by far the best medium since its supple shoots are ideally suited for training into the gently curved tail. The directions here are for a bird surmounting a yew hedge; its silhouette will be seen to advantage in this position or on a freestanding pedestal.

For a bird of the following measurements: height 45cm (18in), length of body 90cm (3ft), length of tail 90cm (3ft); or proportionately.

First year
When clipping the top of the hedge leave a thick tuft of shoots where the pheasant's legs would be. Tie these together in a bundle at the hedge surface using weatherproofed string. Push a stake or thick cane down through the hedge into the ground, or tie a shorter stake to a strong vertical stem in the hedge, so that its top protrudes about 30cm (1ft) above the hedge. Take a piece of stiff fencing wire and bend it as illustrated into the outline of the bird's body, neck and head, then secure it at top and bottom to the stake with thin wire or plastic twine. Bend another piece to define the sides of the body and tie this to the first former. Any shoots that are already long enough can be tied to the wire guide, distributed evenly so that they will gradually fill in the outline, while others are left to grow inside the wires and fill the hollow frame. Select the strongest shoots to train forwards for the neck and head, and back for the tail.

Second year
Continue to tie in the stems up and around the wire body as they grow. Pinch back any shoots growing out from the body to encourage them to branch sideways.

drawing). Tie in the leader of each plant, and if further vertical growth is needed before training starts, shorten any side shoots to about 5cm (2in) long.

Second year (or subsequently if the figures are situated high above the ground)
Unless the figure begins with a straight section (for example, the numbers '1', '7' or '9'), cut off the tip of the leading shoot just above the bottom of the shape. This will force the plant to produce side shoots. Tie in the shoots needed to form the outline, using weatherproofed string, and remove all surplus side shoots below this level to leave a perfectly clean stem.

Third year onwards
Continue to tie in the main structural shoot or shoots to conform to the outline, bending them

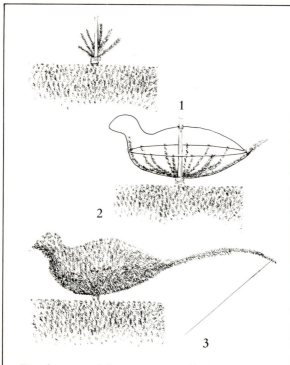

Development of pheasant on top of hedge. **1.** *Bundle of shoots left unclipped and tied to supporting cane.* **2.** *New growth is tied to the shaped former.* **3.** *Nearly completed bird with tail tied down.*

Standing Sheep

Although yew might sound ideal for this subject, Handsworth box is in fact the best choice because of its soft rounded leaves that suggest curls on the fleece, a resemblance that can be emphasized by clipping the head and legs smoother than the rest of the body. A small family group, including lambs shaped from dwarf box, would make an attractive and very appropriate feature on a lawn.

For a sheep 76–90cm (30in–3ft) high.

First year

Prepare an area of ground about 120 x 90cm (4 x 3ft). In the centre of this mark out a rectangle 75 x 30cm (30in x 1ft) and at each corner set a bushy box plant with a supporting cane, to grow as the sheep's legs. After planting trim the sides so that the legs are about 10cm (4in) wide, but leave the tops to grow on.

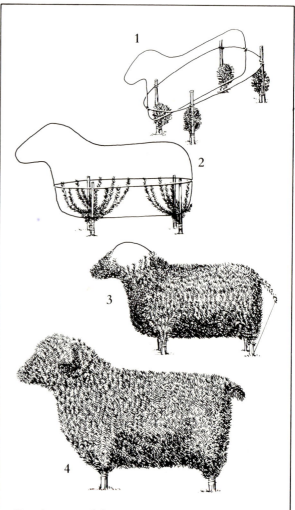

Development of sheep. **1.** *Four plants positioned to form the animal's legs.* **2.** *Growth around base of former.* **3.** *Nearly formed specimen with tail tied down.* **4.** *Finished sheep.*

Third year onwards

When the stems forming the body meet, tie them in to the top wire and pinch out their growing tips. Continue to prevent shoots from growing out from the body, and start to clip the body to shape as the foliage thickens. At the head train the strongest stem down for the pheasant's beak, stop it when long enough and keep its tip bare of foliage.

To form the tail, train two or three stems out behind the body and tie them together. Tie a length of string around the bundle of growth, securing the other end to a strong stem within the hedge to pull the tail downwards — its characteristic curve will develop as the growing stems bend back upwards. When the tail is about half grown, stop all but one of the shoots, allowing this to continue to form the end 'feathers'. To appear in proportion, the tail should be as long as the bird's body. As this single shoot reaches its full length, tie its tip to a peg or weight at ground level to pull the end slightly downwards. When clipping the tail, shape the foliage to taper towards the bare tip of the stem. After a year or two the strings can be removed without fear of the tail springing out of shape.

Clip the pheasant annually in midsummer to prevent too much further growth from blurring its outline before winter.

Second year
Using stiff fencing wire, prepare the formers as illustrated, securing them to the four canes about 30cm (1ft) above the ground. Tie the outer top shoots to the wires to train them around the body, leaving the others to fill the inside.

Third year onwards
Continue to train growth around the framework until it meets at the top, pinching out any shoots that project beyond the body line. Retain a strong shoot at the back, allowing it to grow until it reaches the required size for either a docked or full tail, when it can be pulled down into position with a piece of string secured to the animal's hind legs. Lead the growth at the front to continue around the head former, leaving a couple of side shoots at the top to grow out for the ears. These too might need to be tied down for a season to develop their characteristic forward angle. Once the animal has been shaped,

The classic topiary ornaments are often combined. The centrepiece of this topiary garden, at a wayside shrine in Apulia, Italy, is a swan on a tiered pedestal.

'shear' its fleece annually in midsummer, leaving it to become rough for the rest of the season, but trim the head and legs smooth as often as is necessary to maintain a contrast.

Swan
This can be shaped from any of the usual topiary species and in the past has often formed a decorative feature on the top of a hedge. However, an isolated specimen sitting on the ground and made from golden forms of privet or *Lonicera nitida* would make a brilliant highlight, especially if the design is modified so that the bird 'stands' on two bare stems as legs. For a standing swan, however, the wire frame would have to be tilted up to raise the bird's breast and lower its tail, the shape of its neck might benefit from

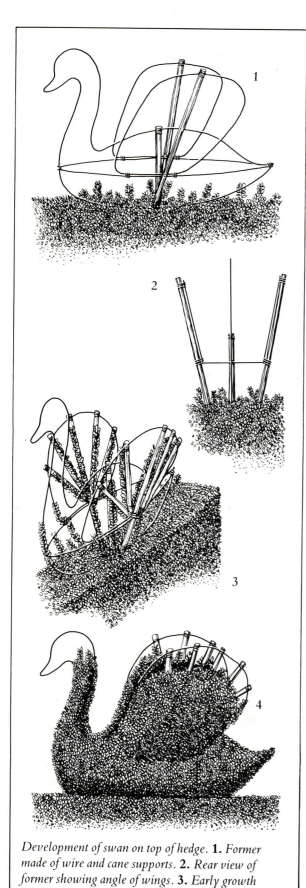

Development of swan on top of hedge. 1. Former made of wire and cane supports. 2. Rear view of former showing angle of wings. 3. Early growth trained along the structure. 4. Swan nearing completion.

slight alteration, and the whole framework would need fixing about 22–30cm (9–12in) above the ground.

First year

For a hedge-top specimen, leave a cluster of shoots unclipped to grow into the body of the swan. (As the bird will be seated, there is no need to bundle the shoots together as for the pheasant.) Prepare wire formers as illustrated and attach the two body wires to a strong vertical stem within the hedge or to a stake pushed firmly into the ground through the hedge. Tie in separate canes to support the wing shapes, each angled slightly outwards, and then tie several thin canes or strings like veins across the wings.

For a freestanding version, plant a single bushy shrub for a sitting swan, or two, side by side and about 30cm (1ft) apart, for a standing bird. Attach wire formers, shaped as above, to plant stakes set in the ground, with additional canes for the wings.

Second year

Trim back any shoots that grow beyond the body, except three or four to be trained up to form the neck and head, and a row of shoots at the base of each wing. Spread these wing shoots out and tie them to the 'veins' on the wire frames, leaving them to grow until they reach the top; there they are tied to the wire and freed from the canes or strings, which can then be removed.

Third year onwards

Continue to trim the body to shape, including the outer edge of the wings to encourage side shoots to fill them out. When the neck stems reach the head, tie them in and then stop all except one which is continued down the bill. When clipping the swan, trim its body, neck and head smooth, but leave a less precise finish at the edges of the wings to suggest the tips of feathers.

Topiary Tiers

The many-tiered 'cake-stand' topiary often seen in cottage gardens is usually carved from older existing trees. However, when this is done branches growing at an angle within the tree usually prevent the slots between tiers from extending right to the trunk, and they are cut only as far as is necessary to give the illusion of separate layers. To reveal the bare main stem between each tier it is almost essential to train a young tree. In this example several tiers are crowned with a grafted split stem, although many other devices such as spheres or simple birds are often used to ornament the top. It will take years to finish the sculpture, but progress will be visible at the end of each season and the developing tree can look attractive from an early stage.

First years of training
Plant a large bushy specimen of yew with a strong stake, and allow it to grow into a small tree. As it develops, shape a round pedestal by clipping a level top about 90cm (3ft) from the ground, using a line stretched horizontally between stakes to ensure a true surface. To shape the outer face of the pedestal, tie one end of a piece of string to the main stem and the other to one handle of a pair of shears the same distance from the stem as the intended radius of the pedestal; with these carefully cut a circular edge to the upper surface. Using this edge as a guide, trim the foliage below to form a cylinder.

Above this pedestal prune away all side shoots to leave 22–30cm (9–12in) of main stem bare. To train the first tier, tie side shoots down until they are horizontal, attaching the other end of the strings to the trunk or to suitably placed branches in the pedestal below. This lowest tier will need to be about 30cm (12in) thick and as wide

as the pedestal — those above can be progressively both thinner and narrower, although remaining the same distance apart. Where enough foliage exists, trim upper surfaces of tiers level and cut the edges clean. Do not expect the undersides of tiers to be covered with foliage, because in the constant shade they will normally remain bare.

Subsequent training
Continue in this way developing a succession of tiers as the tree grows and maintaining as straight a main stem as possible. Above the topmost tier train an enclosed shape around a wire ring, heart or lozenge. This can be done in two ways: either by cutting off the main stem and training two side shoots, one in each direction, to form the outline, grafting the two shoots together again where they meet at the top (see pp.84–85); or, if the stem is long enough to protrude well beyond the top of the ring, by cutting a slit carefully down the middle to produce two half stems that can be tied to each side of the ring with an uncut portion of stem uniting them above the ring. Once the graft has taken, or the split stems hardened to shape, the training ring can be removed. Finish the top of the tree with another full circle made by two shoots trained around a ring that this time is left in place, with the shoots merely stopped at the top.

Development of topiary tiers. **1.** *Shaping of round pedestal with shears attached to stem at desired radius.* **2.** *First tier in formation.* **3.** *Completed specimen crowned by inarchgrafted ring.*

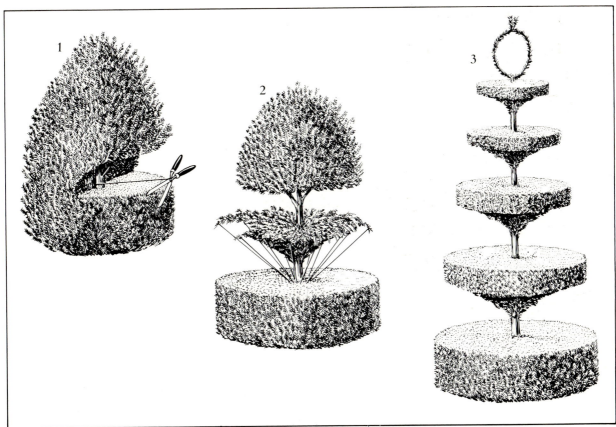

MAINTENANCE

THE ANNUAL ROUTINE

Clipping

Trimming hedges to shape can start immediately after planting (see p.60) and continue annually thereafter, half the season's growth being removed each year to encourage the plants to fill out. As their sides develop, they must be clipped lightly and regularly to encourage them to thicken until the final dimensions of the hedge are reached. With conifers, however, only the ends of side shoots should be lightly tipped; the leaders should be left untouched until they have grown to the required height.

Once established, hedges will need routine clipping, more or less frequently depending on the species and the finish desired. For example, privet can be kept reasonably neat with three clips a year, even fewer if you like the flowers, and yew with only one trim, but if you want sharper, more formal lines, you will have to cut them more often. To clearly define edges and corners, use a line or guide for accuracy at least every other time you clip the hedge (see pp.71–72); if you prefer a softer outline, guides will be needed only once at the beginning of the season, after which you can probably clip by eye.

Always check that the top of the hedge is not growing wider and more vigorously than its base. Unless growth continues long into a mild autumn, stop clipping at the end of the summer to allow young shoots to harden sufficiently to withstand frost later on. The same precaution applies to topiary which, however, may need more frequent clipping to keep the shapes neat — while a flowering privet hedge can be pretty and informal, privet topiary left to bloom looks merely dishevelled.

Where hedges and topiary are enclosed by grass or paths, it should be possible to gather the clippings with a wire rake. Elsewhere, and always with prickly species, spread a large square of sacking or plastic over the ground or neighbouring plants to catch clippings as they fall. Leafy trimmings can be composted, while woodier material needs to be burnt or passed

Clipped Irish yews, variegated holly and a beech hedge bring winter colour to the garden at Barnsley House, Gloucestershire.

through a shredder before composting. Never leave clippings lying around in case they attract fungal diseases such as coral spot as they decay, and spread infection to the living plants. Keep pruning tools sharp, and clean off any sap or debris after use; wipe their blades with an oily cloth before putting them away.

Training and Tying

Where trees have been secured to stakes, make sure the latter are doing their job; often plants are found to be supporting their own stakes if these have rotted or were driven in loosely. Check ties for abrasion on plant stems, and slacken any that threaten to become too tight.

Young growth on trees that are being trained on a frame can develop at a surprising speed. Inspect the plants several times during the growing season and tie shoots in as soon as they are long enough and while still flexible. Check that the string used for earlier ties has not broken, rotted or strangled growth. Make sure, too, that supports on walls have not worked loose.

As the plants mature remove any remaining training ties and supports.

Weeds

Weeds will always try to encroach around the base of hedges and topiary plants. Where there is room, hoe bare soil two or three times during the summer to keep annual weeds in check, and fork out perennials, which will only shoot again if they are merely decapitated. Although mulches prevent many weeds from germinating, any that do appear must be pulled or forked out, since hoeing will be impossible. Tackle weeds promptly: once their roots mingle with those of the shrubs they will be difficult to eradicate.

Pay particular attention to plants with foliage right down to the ground as it is easy to miss weeds growing near their stems — these are ideal situations for the seeds of climbing perennials such as convolvulus, nightshade and bedstraw to lodge and germinate. An alternative to physically removing weeds is to rake in a granular dressing during early spring of a pre-emergent herbicide such as dichlobenil, which will prevent their appearance under woody plants for the whole season. Be careful, though, that you do not apply or rake too much of the chemical around possibly sensitive stems.

Although it is important to prevent trouble-some weeds from growing hidden beneath hedges and topiary, there is no reason why their clipped formality cannot be softened by a few suitable garden plants left to grow at their edges, or perhaps some wild species such as scarlet or blue pimpernel (*Anagallis*), wood violets or ivy-leaved toadflax (*Cymbalaria*). Take care, how-ever, only to allow well-behaved species to take root, or be prepared to ruthlessly confine more adventurous plants like some campanulas or variegated nettles (*Lamium*); trying to remove lemon balm or ivy, for example, where it has grown into a dwarf box hedge could mean sacri-ficing sections of the hedge itself.

If you do let selected flowering plants grow around the base of shrubs, reviving the soil is a useful opportunity to sort them out, cutting back those that have spread, or forking them all out so that you can manure the ground and then replanting young portions of the established clumps. Not all will appreciate this disturbance, especially species which normally colonize dry or waste ground and have hitherto relished the exhausted soil beneath a hedge. But their wel-fare must be secondary to that of the cultivated plants, and they will in any case return in time.

Health
During their early life plants will need feeding annually, and watering whenever a prolonged dry spell sets in. If the weather is hot and dusty, occasionally spray evergreens forcibly with a hose to clean the leaves; do this during the even-ing to avoid leaf scorch from bright sunshine.

Spraying with water will also help to prevent red spider mite from gaining hold. Check for signs of other pests and disease (see pp. 104–105), and watch any plant that fails to thrive. Sometimes the cause is obvious: a locally wet or dry area of ground, for example, can depress growth and if uncorrected may favour a disease such as root rot. If an affected specimen is still young, lift it gently with a fork. Check the con-dition of the soil and notice whether roots are bright and healthy or show signs of decay, often accompanied by an unpleasant smell. Soil pests are rarely a problem on woody plants.

If there is no obvious reason for its malaise, discard the plant. This might seem ruthless, but constitutionally sickly specimens do occur and are seldom worth retaining since they may need constant nursing. It is better to burn such a plant, so preventing the possible spread of a transmissible disease, and then plant a healthy specimen after replacing the soil with a fresh supply from elsewhere in the garden.

Occasionally one or two plants in a young hedge grow more slowly than others, especially if amongst a batch grown from seed, as often happens with yew. This variability is natural and unlikely to be a symptom of ill-health. Leave the slower plants unclipped or only light-ly trimmed in their early years, while cutting the more vigorous ones back to their level until the hedge has a uniform finish.

Winter Care
In regions prone to hard winters, protect topiary by tying up the outer edges to prevent bulging or breakage from snow load; temporary wind-breaks may also be needed in very exposed areas. In more moderate climates it is enough to inspect plants in cold weather, checking that frost has not heaved up the roots of young speci-mens and knocking accumulations of snow from the tops of plants.

Soil Maintenance
Hedges and topiary should be mulched annually with decayed manure and fed early in the grow-ing season with a balanced compound fertilizer.

If, however, in time or through neglect, the soil beneath the plants becomes dusty and ex-hausted, it can be revitalized by lightly forking manure into the surface while the ground is moist. Very often a mat of roots will hinder your working more than superficially. Do not disturb the roots too much; stir in a little of the manure and spread the rest evenly as a mulch.

REPAIRS

Almost inevitably topiary and hedging will suf-fer damage at some time. Dwarf hedges are par-ticularly vulnerable from being trodden on, or knocked by wheelbarrows and garden hoses. Heavy snow left uncleared on the top of plants will often force their sides outwards, while both frost and wind can damage foliage and branches. In most cases repair is possible and new plants will be needed only in extreme cases.

Broken Leaders
Sometimes leading shoots are snapped or in-jured before plants reach their final height. If this happens, a substitute leader must be trained in, especially with conifers whose vertical growth is often checked for a season or two because of their reluctance to replace the damaged shoot. Select a good side shoot near the top of the plant as a replacement leader. Where a portion of the

The start of the maintenance year on formal topiary integrated into an informal garden: the young growth will not need clipping for another couple of months.

Charming as it looks, snow needs prompt removal if its weight is not to distort topiary shapes.

original remains, cut it to leave a piece long enough to tie the replacement into a vertical position alongside. If the leader has broken off completely, tie a short cane to the main stem, allowing the top to protrude a little, and tie the new leader to this.

Frost and Wind Damage

Surface-scorching from frost or wind can be left to grow out and will disappear with clipping. Where a single branch is pushed or falls out of place, as often happens with Irish yews (*Taxus baccata* 'Fastigiata'), either cut it off or tie it back into the body of the tree, securing it to a main stem with plastic twine. If there are plenty of side shoots on the branch it can be severed just inside the face of the tree, and the new growth will quickly conceal the wound. Remove the branch altogether if it is weakened or broken, or where surrounding foliage is dense enough to close around the hole that will be left; this can be encouraged if two or three adjacent branches are tied towards each other over the opening.

Smaller plants that have been knocked or blown out of line can usually be pushed upright again with little trouble. Tread the ground firm around the roots and in dry weather soak thoroughly to settle the disturbed soil once more. They will probably need staking for a season until re-established: support dwarf hedging plants with a discreet cane, or simply by tying to neighbouring plants.

Larger specimens that have been firmly staked at planting are rarely disturbed. If any do blow over, try to find the reason for their weakness before replanting. The roots are unlikely to be diseased without foliar symptoms also being discernible, but inadequate soil preparation might have restricted deeper root development; if so, it will be necessary to improve the soil as for a new specimen (see p.56) before replacing the tree. Sometimes the supporting stake will have rotted or been removed before the tree became self-sufficient, in which case replant with a new stake. In very windy situations either maintain shelter for vulnerable trees or move them to less exposed sites.

Filling Gaps in Hedges

If an entire plant has to be dug up from a hedge due to damage or disease, there are various ways to fill the gap it leaves. One option is to replace it with a new plant. However, the new plant must be approximately the same size as its neighbours if competition is not to depress or distort its growth. Where a replacement is significantly smaller, tie back adjacent branches to admit as much light as possible to the newcomer. For a number of reasons a new plant often refuses to grow well in ground previously occupied by a member of the same species. It is a wise precaution, therefore, to dig out some of the soil from the vacant area and replace it with a fresh supply from elsewhere in the garden.

There may be no need to buy a new plant if those on each side of the gap are close and bushy enough to train towards each other. This is often easily done towards the top of a hedge, but could leave a hole at ground level unless some of the lower branches can be bent without risk of breakage. Tie shoots to each other where they meet, or insert a cane in the centre of the gap and secure them to this. Cut the tips from bent branches to encourage side growth to fill out.

Very flexible lower branches of many species can be pegged down to root as layers in the opening (see p.53). The soil will need improving as for a new plant, and adjacent growth will still have to be tied back to avoid overshadowing the layers. Either cut them free from their parents once they are rooted, or if the join is inconspicuous leave them attached.

To save the purchase of new plants for repairs, and to ensure that replacements are identical with the original hedge, you can extend your stock by taking cuttings (see p.53).

Damage to Stems

The bark at the base of main stems is very vulnerable to injury from being knocked, kicked or gnawed by rabbits and other rodents. If these are a problem, fit expanding spiral guards. Losing a small patch of bark will not harm the tree, but if it is comprehensively stripped around the stem, the tree is in danger of dying because it depends on the tissues just beneath the bark for movement of water and nutrients.

The only possible repair in these extreme cases is a technique known as bridge grafting, by which the bark above and below the girdle of damage is rejoined using defoliated sections taken from one year-old shoots from the same tree. Two of these, positioned opposite each other, will be enough for narrow stems; with a larger tree, one is needed every 2.5cm (1in) or so around its circumference.

Trim the shoots so that they will generously span the injured area, and cut their ends obliquely. Slit the undamaged bark to accommodate the ends of each shoot, and fit the shoots into the slits so that they bridge the injury and bow slightly outwards. Ensure the cut surfaces of the shoots are in contact with the moist layer of tissue beneath the bark. Fix the ends in place with long panel pins or bind them with raffia, and then seal both joins and the stem wound itself with tree-pruning paint. Protect the grafts from damage with a cylinder of wire netting.

PROBLEMS

Die-back

Where bare patches appear in established hedges, cut the dead branches right back to healthy wood (usually paler, moist and soft in texture), even to the main stem itself. Although this may leave an ugly hole, the surrounding foliage will usually grow to fill it, especially if shoots are gently trained across. Where die-back occurs frequently and the hedge has a generally tired appearance, this may be a sign of age or disease (see pp. 104–105). If on further examination the plants seem to be otherwise healthy, the best remedy is usually to cut them back to half their height or even further.

Privet in particular becomes threadbare over the years unless very generously fed, and you should not be afraid to contemplate sawing the whole hedge down to about 30cm (1ft) high. Although this might seem savage treatment, the plants' normal response will be to produce thickets of young, vigorous growth, and these can be thinned to build a new framework of branches.

Die-back may be far more serious in topiary, where the removal of a dead branch may spoil the shape of a specimen. In such cases, consider whether the remaining healthy wood can be pruned to a new or modified shape. The established framework of branches within will make it difficult to shape a new design, but, with little prospect of replacement growth in the near future, the only alternative to recarving the ruined piece would be cutting the plant right back to start afresh.

Sections of hedge inevitably die with age but can be restored either by reshaping or pruning back to stimulate growth.

99

Shading

Hedges can be adversely affected if overshadowed by adjacent trees and taller shrubs. If light is prevented from reaching them, they may become drawn with thin, sparsely leaved shoots, or even die back in places.

If a maturing tree does gradually overshadow a hedge and you are reluctant to thin or restrict its growth, you can help maintain the hedge's good health by recutting its sides to a more pronounced slope (see p.72). This will admit a little more light to the lower branches, which usually suffer most from overshadowing.

It is also worth making this adjustment if a hedge has grown too tall, depriving the branches at its base of light and causing them to become sparse or die back. Clip the lower growth less rigorously than usual, leaving it to extend slowly sideways to compensate for the increased height, and then shape the sides to a new, more oblique angle. Another way to reduce shading at the base is to cut back the shoulders of the hedge, rounding off their sharply defined edges. This will break the angularity of the hedge's outline, a softening effect which could be heightened if the sides were also cut on a slight curve.

RENOVATION OF OVERGROWN TREES AND HEDGES

Occasionally topiary or a hedge is inherited with a new garden, and very often these will be sadly neglected and overgrown. Their restoration, however, can be just as rewarding as creating a finished work from young plants, but inevitably the techniques are different. Instead of training and moulding plants to a preconceived shape, you must rediscover the original form by cutting away surplus growth. Although this will sometimes involve major surgery, young foliage will soon soften the stark outlines and after a few years it will be dense enough for you to start routine clipping. Mature trees that have never been shaped will often tolerate similarly hard pruning to transform them into topiary.

First identify the plants and check in the *Plant Reference Section* (pp. 106–122) that they will stand hard pruning. (Elderly lavender, for example, will often resent being cut back into the old wood, and parts of the plant can die altogether. In such a case it would be wise to abandon the plant and start again with a young replacement.) Decide on the final dimensions of the proposed restoration and be prepared to cut back within this outline, leaving room for young growth to fill out the shape, otherwise you will constantly

be trimming off the leaves back to the framework of old bare wood. This precaution applies to both hedges and topiary. The work is best done in late spring with the worst frosts over and a whole growing season in prospect to ripen new growth.

Topiary

If specimens have been left untrimmed for only a year or two, hard clipping with shears back to their still-discernible outlines will be enough to remove their shagginess; renewal growth will probably make them presentable within a single season. More neglected trees will take longer to reclothe themselves evenly with young foliage, perhaps four years or more, and it will be necessary to cut off some of the more substantial unwanted wood with a saw. As you do this, hold the piece to be removed so that it does not tear as it falls and so produce a ragged wound. Leave all cuts clean to avoid die-back or disease.

When pruning a tree hard do the work in stages, cutting gradually from all sides. Stand back frequently to make sure you are not removing too much, for it is easy to destroy the symmetry of a tree by over-enthusiasm. Try to conform as far as possible to the original shape of a piece of former topiary; alterations to the inner framework could unbalance the tree or leave a gaping hole that will take years to fill. Never trust your eye where corners or flat faces are to be recut, but use a guide.

Hedges

Gardeners often need to renovate or reduce the size of a hedge, and the same principles apply as to topiary trees. For much of the work you will need secateurs (hand pruners) and loppers or a saw, rather than shears, and if the hedge is large you will need to set up a stable platform on steps or trestles.

It is best to start by reducing the height — unless extensive side growth restricts access, in which case one side will have to be cut back first. Cut 2.5–5cm (1–2in) or so below the final level on dwarf hedges, up to 30cm (1ft) lower with taller ones. Where you have or intend a freely undulating finish, as with wide yew banks, surplus growth can be removed by eye. Avoid any sudden changes in direction and proceed slowly: more wood can always be removed after you have assessed your progress.

To keep tops and sides level you will need guide lines, set up as described on pp.71–72. At this stage it is usually possible to estimate the perpendicularity or slope of the side as you go, because the face can be clipped true once enough renewal growth has been made.

The sides of many hedging plants may be cut right back to the main stems if necessary, but if you intend to prune as severely as this, leave the second side until the following year to avoid too great a shock to the plants. Where less than half the depth of each side is to be cut off, both can be done at the same time. Finish one side before starting the other. Immediately after hard pruning, spur plants into growth with a dressing of general fertilizer around their roots or a mulch of decayed manure when the soil is moist.

RESHAPING ESTABLISHED HEDGES

Though an established hedge might appear to be permanent and unalterable, there is no reason why, with care, it should not be clipped to a new shape. Not only is it possible — and sometimes beneficial — to cut the sides to a new angle; ornamental alterations, both structural and superficial, may also be made.

Beware of altering the shape of a healthy established hedge too drastically: as ever, you should be conscious of the framework of branches beneath the enveloping foliage. If by thoughtless pruning one or two trees within a hedge are left out of true, they will always try to restore the balance, producing excessively

Restoration in progress at Canons Ashby, Northamptonshire. Top: overgrown yews. Centre: the same trees after severe pruning, with surrounding turf removed to reduce competition. Bottom: clipped new growth four years after reduction.

A yew hedge is clipped into pinnacles at Nymans, Sussex. With shaping and retraining, a plain solid hedge could be transformed into a similarly decorative feature.

vigorous growth in some directions, while refusing to fill out in others.

Simple designs can be incorporated into hedges of many species, including deciduous plants such as beech and hornbeam. While a tall overgrown hedge of these is unlikely to have stems straight or evenly spaced enough for you to shave the foliage from the lower portion and so produce a stilt hedge, you might be able to form buttresses along the sides, shape the ends into taller and wider columns, or gently undulate the top (see also p. 40).

Overgrown yew hedges offer unlimited possibilities, especially for the addition of topiary ornaments on the top. One traditional geometrical decoration for the top of a yew hedge is crenellation, with square blocks of foliage removed at regular intervals. Very accurate distances and angles must be maintained if it is not to look amateurish, even though dense, level faces will not be achieved for three or four years, until new foliage has fully covered the cut surfaces. Where the trees are suitably spaced, it might be possible to cut a window or doorway into the side of a tall hedge, opening up a previously concealed vista, or even make an arcade. Accuracy is again very important here: the sides of an arch or doorway must appear to be upright, the top evenly curved or parallel with the ground or top of the hedge, or whichever level is more conspicuous should they differ. Shapes of this type must ultimately be cut by eye, although guides, such as a pair of tall canes rested against the face of the hedge to mark a doorway, can make the job a little easier.

MOVING LARGE TREES

If the job is done properly, quite large trees can be transplanted in the garden. This can be important for the topiarist since it makes it possible to resite an already sizeable specimen in a new position before conversion into topiary — a valuable short cut if you want topiary in a particular place. It may also prevent the loss of years of hard work if a specimen has, for one reason or another, outgrown its allotted space; in such a case, always consider the feasibility of moving a tree as an alternative to felling it or cutting it right back.

To give a tree the best chance of surviving a move, it is important to cut out as large a root ball as possible, and to keep this from disintegrating *en route*. To hold the ball intact a number of hessian (burlap) sacks will be needed, cut down one side and along the bottom so that they open out flat. Make a large square by joining four or more, roughly stitching them together with a thick needle and plastic twine.

Mark a circle on the ground around the tree, preferably at the outer limits of its branches but no more than 1–1.25m (3–4ft) in diameter otherwise it will be extremely heavy to lift. If you can plan well ahead, mark out this circle during the dormant season a year before moving the tree, and dig down two spits deep along this line to cut through the lateral roots. Replace the soil, water, and leave until the following year, when fibrous roots will have grown around the edge of the circle.

If this is not practicable, all the work will have to be done at the time of moving. Make sure the soil is moist, otherwise it will fall away from the roots when lifted. Loop string around spreading branches and tie them in out of the way. While digging around the circle, cut or saw any main roots cleanly at both sides of the trench. Throw the soil clear so that you have plenty of room in which to work. When the trench is about 60cm (2ft) deep, clean out any loose soil and then, from one side first of all, start to undercut the root ball by digging towards the trunk of the tree, sliding out the soil and cutting any roots you encounter.

Moving large trees. **1.** *Tree with foliage tied in.* **2.** *Sacking unrolled beneath partly undercut root ball.* **3.** *Fully excavated tree.* **4.** *Root ball wrapped and ready for transportation.*

When you get to a point roughly half-way across, clear all loose soil and make sure you can reach under the root ball with your arm as far as you have dug. Take the sacking square and roll half up tightly to the centre. Tuck the roll under the root ball as far as it will go, leaving the unrolled area of sacking spread out evenly beneath the excavated roots with enough around the sides to fold over and tie close to the trunk.

Now start digging horizontally from the opposite side, again cutting any roots cleanly, until you reach the rolled-up sacking. Tilting the tree away from you, pull this roll through and spread it beneath the rest of the root ball. Wrap the sacking up around the ball and secure it by tying opposite corners firmly together with string. With plenty of help, because it will be heavy, you can then lift the tree out of its hole and carry it to the new site. For very heavy trees you may have to dig a slope down to the bottom of the hole, and either ease the ball on to a trolley or simply drag it up and across the ground.

Where necessary, the balled tree can stand in a sheltered place for a few weeks, especially if the ball is covered with soil or mulch for frost protection. However, it is always best to plant straight away. Have the ground prepared and a large-enough hole dug beforehand. Decide on the best way round for the tree to be planted so that there is no need to adjust it once in place, and lower it into the hole.

Cut away the sacking, leaving the disc of material beneath the ball to rot. Fill in the hole, treading the soil very firmly as you go, and finish off level. The tree will need support for a few years and must either be staked or guyed with three or four thin ropes. Finally, cut the strings encircling the foliage and give the ground a generous mulch to feed roots and reduce aftercare.

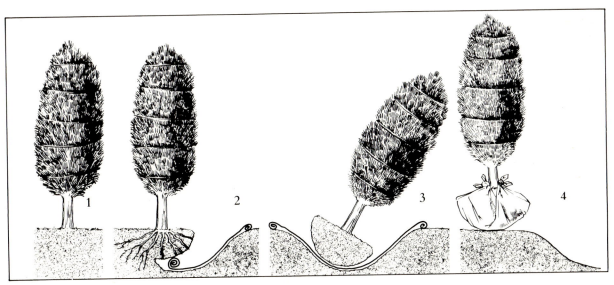

PESTS AND DISEASES

In addition to the plants it contains, a healthy garden is a thriving community of insects and micro-organisms. Sometimes gardeners become over-sensitive about this and assume every insect is a pest or that marks on a leaf are necessarily symptoms of disease, whereas it must be stressed that only a minority of these are positively harmful. In a flourishing garden disorders are surprisingly few and infrequent.

Where trouble is likely, prevention is nearly always better than cure, although this does not mean you have to maintain a constant programme of precautionary spraying throughout the season. It is in fact dangerous to continually drench plants with chemicals.

Not only do the real pests and diseases quickly acquire immunity to fungicides and pesticides that are in frequent use, but countless beneficial species are also affected by many of the popular chemical sprays.

Aim for positive health by preparing the ground carefully in the first place and keeping plants in good condition thereafter. They will then be fit enough to resist or at least to tolerate potential disorders. Many of these, such as die-back or yellowing leaves, may in any case be no more than symptoms of distress caused by poor cultivation; others are infections that thrive as a result of neglect, for example coral spot and sooty mould.

The main pests and diseases likely to affect hedges and topiary plants are

briefly listed here, together with suitable basic remedies. (For fuller details and information on rarer or more specific ailments consult a specialist handbook.) The treatments suggested here are least likely to be toxic to other garden life, especially insects that prey on the pests concerned. Ironically, while many insects and fungi have already developed strains resistant to some of the more toxic modern chemicals, they remain vulnerable to simpler and more traditional remedies. Always spray either in the cool of the evening or very early in the morning when pollinating insects are not at work, and avoid spraying open blooms. To prevent injury to plants or beneficial insects, always follow the manufacturer's instructions carefully.

Greenfly

Woolly aphis

Caterpillar

Froghopper (spittle bug)

Leaf Miner

Red spider mite

Scale insect

Whitefly

Coral spot

Rust

Sooty mould

INSECT PESTS

Aphids (Greenfly, Blackfly, Woolly Aphis etc). This is an enormous group of small insects that feed on a plant's sap. The winged forms colonize soft shoots, buds and the undersides of leaves, and soon produce wingless generations that rapidly spread the infestation. Probably the most common seasonal garden pests, causing distortion of leaves and shoots and, more seriously, sometimes spreading virus diseases. They also produce sticky deposits of honeydew. They are more likely to trouble plants grown 'soft' with overfeeding. Woolly aphis can heavily infest new growth on box. Spray at an early stage with insecticidal soap or soapy water (a mixture of 1–2 tablespoons washing-up liquid to 4 ltr/ 1 US gal water), or with a suitable insecticide such as derris or pyrethrum (pyrethrin).

Caterpillars. The larvae of a wide variety of moths and butterflies will feed on the leaves of many trees and shrubs. Either pick them off whenever seen or, if there are too many, spray with derris or *Bacillus thuringiensis*, a fungal preparation that affects only caterpillars.

Froghoppers (Spittle Bugs). Green, brown, or red and black, jumping insects usually first noticed by the masses of froth ('cuckoo spit') they produce on young shoots. The shoots may later become distorted, but otherwise these insects are relatively harmless; either ignore them or spray forcefully with a garden hose.

Leaf Miners. Grubs that tunnel within leaf tissues, leaving pale and meandering trails. Pick off affected leaves and burn or crush.

Red Spider Mite. Minute creatures, not strictly spiders at all, which feed on plant tissues, producing yellow speckling and a bronze sheen on leaves, followed later by fine webs strung between leaves and their shoots. The mites are more prevalent in very warm weather and an epidemic of them is often a result of excessively dry conditions. Spray with an insecticide such as derris and also forcefully drench foliage with a hose whenever watering in the evening.

Scale Insects. Small, sap-feeding insects that normally hide under hard, rounded scales on stems or the undersides of leaves. Their eggs are often laid beneath a covering of white waxy wool. Can be common on beech, bay and yew. In the UK, relatively harmless, but types found in North America can be more damaging. Like aphids, scale insects produce honeydew. They are difficult to treat. Inspect all new woody plants for characteristic scales, and wipe any off with a sponge and soapy water. Spray in late spring with pyrethrum (pyrethrin) as unprotected juveniles move around the plant in search of new feeding grounds. Where infestation is serious, spray with carbaryl (sevin) or, in North America, with acethate or superior oil.

Whitefly. Small insects, pure white and delta-shaped, that feed on the undersides of leaves and fly up suddenly at the slightest disturbance. Their young are seen as tiny white scales stuck to the leaf surface. Spray with pyrethrum (pyrethrin) during early summer.

DISEASES

Coral Spot. A fungus that primarily colonizes dead wood, covering its surface with a speckling of tiny coral-pink pustules, but can also invade living branches causing their death. Best avoided by pruning out any dead wood and burning it. Never leave clippings lying around to become a reservoir of infection.

Fireblight. Bacterial infection, serious in North America and becoming so in areas of Britain, that kills flowers and leaves on affected shoots which themselves eventually die back to leave an appearance of having been scorched by fire. It affects members of the Rosaceae (e.g. pyracantha, cotoneaster, hawthorn) and is becoming a considerable threat to fruit orchards. The only remedy is to prune back to unaffected wood, dipping secateurs (hand pruners) frequently in strong disinfectant during and after the operation; or to remove and burn seriously affected shrubs. (In some areas of the UK fireblight is a notifiable disease: report suspected infections to the Ministry of Agriculture.)

Honey Fungus (Bootlace Fungus). Young trees can be killed and older ones seriously disabled by this fungus, which normally spreads through the soil from dead tree stumps by means of dark threads, like bootlaces. Toadstools, usually honey-coloured, appear in autumn on infected tree trunks within about 60cm (2ft) from the ground. Accurate diagnosis and effective treatment are difficult, and both are matters for professional advice. Proprietory chemicals can sometimes prevent infection but seldom cure diseased trees. Some species, such as beech, box, holly and yew, seem to be resistant to the fungus; cypress, chamaecyparis and privet are highly susceptible.

Mildews. Parasitic fungi that produce powdery or slimy white deposits on leaves and stems, eventually inhibiting growth and causing plants to sicken generally. At an early stage pick off all infected leaves and spray with benomyl or a mixture of 85g (3oz) washing soda and a handful of soap flakes dissolved in 4ltr (1 US gal) hot water and allowed to cool.

Root Rots. Common diseases whose first symptoms above ground are sudden yellowing of leaves, followed by extensive die-back and even total collapse. If an affected plant is dug up, its roots will often appear black and decayed. Although caused by soil fungi these rots are often encouraged by poor drainage and insufficient feeding. The correction of nutrient and drainage deficiencies may cure the problem, but if this fails the plants should be destroyed.

Rusts. A large group of fungi that cause yellow spotting on the tops of leaves. On the undersides, red, orange or brown pustules appear, containing spores which will spread the infection to other leaves, particularly in wet weather. Pick off rusty leaves carefully and burn, and spray affected plants with a copper fungicide or general protectant fungicide. Avoid spraying when young growth is present and take care to protect any herbaceous plants in the vicinity. Clean away all fallen leaves from affected plants.

Sooty Mould. Sooty black fungus that colonizes the sticky honeydew secreted by aphids and other insects. It is disfiguring rather than harmful, and will eventually disappear if the insects producing the honeydew are controlled.

Artemisia

Azara

Berberis

Carpinus

Buxus

Caryopteris

Cephalotaxus

Cassinia

Chaenomeles

Chamaecyparis

Corylus

Cotoneaster

PLANT REFERENCE SECTION

The plants described on the following pages are all accepted media for one or more forms of topiary, and can be reliably recommended. However, this selection by no means exhausts the range of possible subjects for clipping: many plants are more adaptable than gardeners appreciate, and it is worth exploring the suitability of other varieties or species. Entries are listed alphabetically by botanical name, while alternative common names are cross-referenced in the index.

The description of each plant is followed by a brief guide to cultivation. Gardeners should note that the suggested timings for planting and pruning are not inflexible, and will in practice be governed by the weather and condition of the soil, or the amount of growth that has been made. Similarly, ultimate sizes given for hedges and topiary are approximate, depending in reality on many factors such as aspect and situation, quality of plants, and the amount of attention given to training and cultivation.

Geographical location and average winter temperatures also profoundly affect a plant's performance. Each variety listed is given a rating for winter hardiness (indicated by a figure in brackets) according to the scale determined by the United States Department of Agriculture (see table). This scale was initially devised for North America, dividing the continent into 'hardiness zones' based upon the range of minimum temperatures in a typical winter. It has since been extended to Europe, including Britain (whose peculiar island climate makes it roughly classifiable as zone 8 with small areas of zones 7 and 9). The system is increasingly becoming accepted as a useful guide to a plant's chances of long-term survival within a given region. However, it is no more than a convenient approximation. In any garden local conditions such as exposure to wind and summer sunshine, altitude or freedom from frosts in early autumn are often more critical considerations for plants of borderline hardiness.

Zone	Minimum temperature range	
	°C	°F
1	below −45	below −50
2	−45 to −40	−50 to −40
3	−40 to −34	−40 to −30
4	−34 to −29	−30 to −20
5	−29 to −23	−20 to −10
6	−23 to −17	−10 to 0
7	−17 to −12	0 to 10
8	−12 to −7	10 to 20
9	−7 to −1	20 to 30
10	−1 to −5	30 to 40

ARTEMISIA

Shrubby aromatic deciduous cottage-garden plants, introduced to Britain from southern Europe in the sixteenth century. Lad's love or southernwood, *A. abrotanum* (6) is the best species, hardy and growing naturally to about 90cm (3ft) but often clipped as a low hedge in knot gardens or for edging beds of herbs. The erect stems are covered with finely divided leaves, downy and silvery-grey. Plants need full sun for the best colour but will tolerate urban atmospheres and poor soils. Yellow button-like flowers are produced in late summer, although clipping usually prevents these from forming.

Plant bushy container-grown specimens 30cm (12in) apart in autumn or spring. Cut to shape in early spring before growth starts and trim lightly with shears as necessary thereafter. Propagate by semi-ripe cuttings in a shady bed outdoors in midsummer.

AZARA

Evergreen shrubs with small shiny leaves and fragrant though insignificant yellowish-green flowers in spring. They prefer light, well-drained soil and shelter from cold wind. The hardiest species is the neat *A. microphylla* (8) with elegant growth that can be trained as small espaliers on a wall or clipped into a low hedge in mild districts; leaves of the slower growing *A. m.* 'Variegata' have pretty cream markings.

For hedges up to about 120cm (4ft), plant 30cm (12in) apart in autumn or spring. Prune to shape in spring until the final outline has developed, when one or two light clips each season will maintain a clean finish. For espaliers, train in the required stems, cleanly removing any growing out from the wall and shortening all others to 5cm (2in) long.

Propagate by semi-ripe cuttings in late summer in a cold frame or, in very cold areas, in a frost-free greenhouse.

BERBERIS (BARBERRY)

Very hardy evergreen and deciduous shrubs that thrive with little attention in any well-drained soil inland or beside the sea. Evergreen kinds are decorative all the year round and with regular clipping these make dense and impenetrable thorny hedges. Deciduous berberis can make even denser, more prickly hedges with brilliant colours in autumn.

If flowers and berries are required, plants must be grown informally, although a few will appear even on strictly clipped hedges. Most species and cultivars are suitable for hedging, but not all have interesting foliage. Among the best are:

B. buxifolia 'Nana' (6) — dense masses of small evergreen leaves, grey underneath, on slow-growing plants that seldom exceed 45cm (18in) in height. Plant 15–25cm (6–9in) apart and trim in spring.

B. calliantha (5) — holly-like evergreen leaves, blue-white beneath, on stems that are red when young; has wide-spreading, suckering habit up to

60–90cm (2–3ft). Plant 45–60cm (8–24in) apart, and trim as necessary in spring and midsummer.

B. darwinii (7) — dark shiny evergreen leaves. Makes an attractive flowering hedge, with racemes of deep golden blooms in late spring. Can reach 150cm (5ft) or more in height, but will make a denser hedge if kept down to around 60cm (2ft); flowering will be reduced by clipping. Plant 45–60cm (18–24in) apart. Trim after flowering and again in late summer.

B. gagnepainii (6) — dense, erect evergreen with dark narrow leaves. Very spiny and makes an impenetrable hedge up to 180cm (6ft) high or more. Plant 45cm (18in) apart and trim in late spring and summer.

B. julianae (6) — very dense and spiny with hard narrow leaves, copper when young. Makes an impenetrable evergreen hedge or screen to 180cm (6ft) high or more. Plant 60cm (2ft) apart and clip in late spring and summer.

B. panlanensis (6–7) — compact evergreen growth with toothed sea-green leaves. Makes a neat low hedge up to 45cm (18in) high. Plant 15–25cm (6–9in) apart and trim in summer.

B. thunbergii (4) — compact deciduous species with brilliant autumn colours. Makes a hardy impenetrable hedge up to 90–120cm (3–4ft), less dense at greater height. The form *B.t. atropurpurea* and the cultivar *B.t.* 'Atropurpurea Nana' have reddish-purple foliage that turns scarlet in autumn, and make ideal coloured hedges 90cm (3ft) and 60cm (2ft) high respectively. *B.t.* 'Erecta' is an upright green form with vivid autumn colours, producing a dense narrow hedge up to 90cm (3ft) high. Plant all these kinds 40cm (15in) apart and trim in spring and summer.

To prevent excessive vertical growth at the expense of side shoots, cut berberis back half-way after planting, and trim the top as well as the sides each year until full height is reached. When trimming in subsequent years, thin some of the older shoots to make way for young growth from the base. If the sides of established plants become bare at the base, rejuvenate the hedge by cutting it right down to a few centimetres high in early spring.

Because of their thorns, great care is needed when weeding beneath berberis hedges, and the use of a persistent granular herbicide is recommended. On all but the best soils, feed with a general balanced fertilizer each year in spring.

Propagate berberis either by semi-ripe cuttings in a cold frame outdoors in autumn, or by lifting plants and separating them into smaller divisions for replanting.

BUXUS (BOX)

For centuries one of the most popular evergreen topiary and hedging plants, hardy in most areas and tolerant of all soils and sites except where drainage is poor. The tough, neat foliage stands constant clipping, and overgrown plants respond to severe pruning, although the old wood is extremely hard to cut.

Several forms of box are valuable for hedges and topiary. The most useful are:

B. microphylla (little-leaf box) (6) —a dense dwarf species with a rounded habit and small leaves narrower than those of common box. The best form is the bright green American clone 'Green Pillow', compact and slow growing to about 60cm (2ft) high after ten years or so. This makes a neat dwarf hedge for knot gardens, needing only occasional clipping to shape. Plant container-grown specimens 15–25cm (6–9in) apart.

B. sempervirens (common box) (6) — the box normally used for clipped work. The species, with rounded deep-green foliage, will grow naturally into a small tree after many years. It has given rise to many forms, the best of which for large topiary is 'Handsworthensis', very vigorous and erect with thick dark-green leaves. This can be grown and trained up to 3m (10ft) or more as a hedge or screen, or for specimen topiary.

The variegated forms of *B. sempervirens* are very decorative but less vigorous than 'Handsworthensis': 'Elegantissima' is dense and compact with green leaves edged white; 'Aureovariegata' is slightly larger with yellow mottled markings; and 'Gold Tip' has variable yellow-tipped leaves

on the upper shoots. For hedges plant all these kinds 60cm (2ft) apart, using plants about 45cm (18in) tall.

The best dwarf forms of *B. sempervirens* are 'Latifolia Maculata', dense and compact with large leaves irregularly marked with yellow splashes; and the venerable 'Suffruticosa' (edging box), with shiny bright-green leaves. Hedges of these kinds are best kept well below their maximum height of 90cm (3ft), although with care specimen topiary can be trained a little taller. Both kinds stand frequent clipping and also hard pruning in late spring. Plant bushy specimens 15cm (6in) apart.

To ensure healthy plants, the soil must be enriched prior to planting, and hedges should be fed annually with either a balanced fertilizer or a light mulch of rotted manure; take care the latter does not encourage slugs and snails to shelter amongst the congested stems. Box roots spread as a dense mat sideways for some distance into cultivated soil; for the sake of neighbouring plants it is wise to cut through the soil with a spade 7–10cm (3–4in) from the sides of a hedge every few years to sever these invasive roots.

Propagate box by semi-ripe cuttings taken in autumn, from the same plant if consistent colour is important, rooting them in a frame outdoors or a greenhouse.

CARPINUS (HORNBEAM)

Versatile and easily grown deciduous trees, flourishing on most soils including clay, and in exposed situations. The leaves are slightly rough, strongly veined and serrated at the edges, but otherwise resemble those of beech. Their naturally dense habit responds well to pollarding and clipping, to produce hedges from about 120cm (4ft) up to 6m (20ft) or more high, while the long flexible growth is ideal for pleaching. Formally trimmed hedges retain their dead leaves until the following spring in the same way as beech; compared with the latter, however, clipped hornbeam develops a denser face of fine twigs. With their attractive grey bark, smooth at first but becoming fluted with age, the trunks are sometimes left exposed at the base of stilt hedges.

Two kinds are usually grown: *C. caroliniana* (American hornbeam) **(2)**, a spreading tree with bright apple-green foliage, and *C. betulus* (common hornbeam) **(4)**, darker-leaved and more vigorous. Several forms of the latter are available, but the only ones useful for hedging are *C.b.* 'Fastigiata' and the rarer 'Variegata' whose leaves are variably marked with creamy-white patches.

For hedging choose dormant young trees 30–45cm (12–18in) tall, either bare-rooted or container-grown. Plant 45–60cm (18–24in) apart and leave unpruned for two seasons. For pollarding, pleaching and stilt hedges, plant taller specimens 180cm–3m (6–10ft) apart and stake securely, tying in the leading shoot and shortening all others to half their length after planting. Prune in winter when dormant and clip in summer, not during the spring when trees can bleed excessively.

Propagate by layering or from seed, although this often takes two years to germinate.

CARYOPTERIS (BLUEBEARD)

Low deciduous shrubs with grey fragrant leaves, growing best in light well-drained ground and a sunny position. They will stand clipping to shape and make a neat hedge 45–60cm (18in–2ft) high, especially on chalky soils, although regular clipping will prevent the attractive blue flowers from developing in late summer onwards.

For hedging, plant 30cm (12in) apart cultivars of the hybrid *C.* × *clandonensis* **(5)** such as 'Kew Blue' or 'Arthur Simmonds' (both bright blue) or the American clone 'Heavenly Blue' (deeper blue). Trim to shape in early spring, cutting back almost to the old wood, and clip occasionally thereafter. If flowers are required stop clipping at midsummer.

Propagate by soft cuttings from an early summer trim, or semi-ripe cuttings in midsummer.

CASSINIA

Dense evergreen foliage shrubs, most of which bear small leaves that look golden *en masse*. They prefer a site with well-drained soil and either full sun or light shade. One of the best-known species is *C. fulvida* (sometimes called *Diplopappus chrysophyllus*) **(8)** excellent for a low clipped hedge 90cm (3ft) high and particularly useful in coastal gardens.

Plant 30cm (12in) apart and trim the young growth whenever necessary during the summer. If left to grow as an informal hedge, plants will bear dense heads of white flowers in July.

Propagate in autumn by semi-ripe cuttings in a frame outdoors.

CEPHALOTAXUS (PLUM YEW)

Evergreen conifers closely resembling yew, although the leaves are generally a little larger. They grow in most soils and situations, even in shade. One species, *C. harringtonia drupacea* (Japanese plum yew) **(6)** is sometimes grown for clipping into low mounds in gardens designed with an oriental style. It has smaller leaves than most other related species and naturally forms a compact shrub, suitable for low dense hedges.

Cultivation details as for yew (see *Taxus*).

CHAENOMELES (FLOWERING QUINCE)

Deciduous thorny shrubs, very hardy and tough in most situations. Decorative and painfully impenetrable as formal hedges 90–180cm (3–6ft) high when clipped immediately after flowering and again in midsummer, also attractive as espaliers.

C. japonica (Japanese quince) **(5)** is a small species (under 90cm/3ft) with brilliant orange flowers. *C. speciosa* (popularly known as japonica) **(4)** is more vigorous and branching. The species usually has bright red flowers, although the shade is variable in plants grown from seed. There are numerous cultivars of this, or hybrids between these two species and others; all are very decorative but have different habits. 'Simonii', for example, has crimson flowers and grows little more than 90cm (3ft) tall, whereas the stout hybrid 'Crimson and Gold' will reach 3m (10ft). Make sure, therefore, that the chosen variety matches its proposed use.

Always plant container-grown specimens to avoid root disturbance, which these plants resent. For hedges plant 30–45cm (12–18in) apart during dormancy.

Chaenomeles are easily trained with support as espaliers against a wall; prune plants after flowering by shortening side shoots growing parallel with the wall to three or four leaves. In summer remove any shoots growing out from the wall, or shorten to two or three leaves if they are to be retained. Remove suckers at the base of trained plants before they become large and woody. Pears and edible quinces can be budded in summer on to a chaenomeles hedge to form fruiting trees (see p. 85).

Propagate by seed sown outdoors in spring; layering; semi-ripe cuttings in summer; or budding named cultivars on to seedling root stocks. (Seedlings seldom come true to type.)

CHAMAECYPARIS (FALSE CYPRESS)

Evergreen conifers of distinctive conical shape, with flattened branchlets of small scaly leaves and long whip-like stems; ideal for hedging since frequent clipping improves their density provided they are not cut back into old wood. They will survive on dry or shallow soils, but prefer moist open ground that is well-drained. Grey and gold forms possess the best resistance to wind and sea spray.

Many good forms have been developed, although most are best as specimen trees. The most useful tree for hedging is *C. lawsoniana* (Lawson cypress) **(6)**, a large sturdy tree with pendulous sombre foliage. There are numerous cultivars, of which the most outstanding are:
C.l. 'Fletcheri' — dense compact columnar shape, with feathery grey-green foliage. Fairly slow growth. Makes an attractive hedge up to 120–150cm (4–5ft) tall.
C.l. 'Green Hedger' — dense rich-green foliage, branching freely from the base. A little more expensive than some, because it has to be propagated

from cuttings. Eventual height of hedge 3–4.5m (10–15ft).

C.l. 'Stewartii' — an elegant golden-yellow form that develops a greenish tinge during winter months. Very hardy and useful for hedges up to 2.5–3m (8–10ft).

Plant hedges during autumn or spring, choosing small plants about 45cm (18in) tall and setting them 45–60cm (18–24in) apart in a single row. Trim side shoots back with secateurs (hand pruners) until the hedge is developed, when shears can be used, first in early spring and again during the season when necessary. To avoid bare patches at the base trim hedges with a batter. Unlike many conifers which resent root disturbance, chamaecyparis can be planted as bare-root stock and tolerate being moved even as small established trees.

Propagate from semi-ripe cuttings in autumn in a frame or a greenhouse.

CORYLUS (HAZEL, FILBERT)

Hardy deciduous shrubs with large rounded leaves that turn bright yellow in autumn, and attractive male catkins in spring. Hazel is ideal for combining with beech, hornbeam etc., or grown on its own as a hedge up to 3m (10ft) or more; this is best trained as a plashed or 'laid' hedge in traditional style (see p.73). Plants thrive in almost any type of soil and situation other than deep shade.

C. avellana (common or European hazel) **(4)** — a large shrub or small tree with several stems, which can be left to form a tall informal fruiting screen up to 6m (20ft) high. For this prune out during spring any very old wood and shorten younger stems by a third. In a mixed hedge clip with shears as necessary. *C.a.* 'Aurea' is a pale yellow cultivar, but not as robust as the species.

C. maxima (filbert, giant filbert) **(5)** — with heart-shaped leaves, best known in gardens for its form *C.m.* 'Purpurea', whose leaves are an intense rich purple that makes a spectacular contrast with golden hazel. Hedges 180cm–3m (6–10ft) high.

Plant about 45cm (18in) apart any time between autumn and spring.

Propagate by layering in summer, or by digging up suckers or sowing nuts in autumn.

COTONEASTER

A large group of evergreen and deciduous shrubs, many of which are suitable for formally clipped and informal flowering hedges, a few also making excellent decorative espaliers on walls. Most are very hardy and tolerant of all soils. Of the numerous species and cultivars the following are particularly attractive.

C. franchetii **(7)** — graceful, semi-evergreen shrub of medium vigour, leaves green above when mature with white or buff felted undersides; produces white flowers in spring and bright orange-scarlet oval berries in autumn. Plant 45cm (18in) apart for hedges up to 250cm (8ft) high, or as specimens for espaliers.

C. microphyllus **(7)** — dwarf evergreen with small dark shiny green leaves; large scarlet berries. Has very tough constitution and makes an excellent low hedge up to 60cm (2ft) high. Plant 30cm (12in) apart.

C. salicifolius **(6)** — tall, graceful evergreen with wrinkled dark shiny leaves and heavy crops of bright red berries; can reach 4.5m (15ft) high in ten years. Plant 60cm (2ft) apart for a hedge up to 3m (10ft), or singly against walls for large espaliers.

C. simonsii **(6)** — semi-evergreen shrub with dense erect growth, whose dark glossy leaves assume bright autumn tints; large scarlet fruits in autumn. Very hardy and tough. Plant 45cm (18in) apart for a hedge up to 180cm (6ft), which can be trimmed down to only 30cm (12in) thick. Also makes attractive espaliers.

Plant all cotoneasters between autumn and spring. Clipped as hedges, in early spring and again later if necessary, bushes will develop few berries. If these are required, trim in spring (prune espalier side shoots to three to five leaves) and then allow to flower, later pruning back any growth that forms beyond the developing fruits.

Propagate by semi-ripe cuttings in a cold frame in late summer or early autumn, or seeds in a cold frame in autumn.

CRATAEGUS (HAWTHORN)

Hardy deciduous spiny shrubs which grow vigorously in almost any soil and situation, tolerating frequent formal clipping, when they assume a very neat appearance, and hard cutting back where necessary. Traditionally grown on its own and plashed to form impenetrable boundary hedges (see p.73), but can also be mixed with other deciduous species. Ornamental flowering varieties can be budded as specimen trees on to common hedging species (see p.85).

C. monogyna (common or English hawthorn, may, quickthorn) **(5)** — the best hedging species, with fragrant white flowers in spring and red haws in autumn, although few of either appear when hedges are clipped formally. Useful for hedges up to 3–3.5m (10–12ft). The forms 'Variegata' with leaves splashed creamy-white, and 'Compacta', an erect dwarf variety without thorns, are both valuable alternatives for hedging, though rarer and more expensive than the species.

C. laevigata (syn. *oxyacantha*) **(5)** — similar to the above, although less commonly planted.

C. phaenopyrum (Washington thorn) **(5)** — unusual for its glossy maple-like leaves and brilliant autumn tints.

Buy plants 30–45cm (12–18in) tall (preferably transplanted once in the nursery), and set them 30–45cm (12–18in) apart in single rows between autumn and spring. Cut back to about 15cm (6in) high as soon as growth begins the first spring. Trim hedges in early June and thereafter as necessary, including a last clip in autumn to reduce the number of mildew spores that overwinter in the outer buds.

Propagate by seed, sown in autumn for exposure to frost; layering in late spring; budding in early summer.

× CUPRESSOCYPARIS

A small group of hybrid conifers, the most important of which is *C. leylandii* (Leyland cypress) **(6)**, an extremely fast growing dense plant which flourishes almost anywhere including windy and coastal sites. Trees have flattened

Crataegus

× Cupressocyparis

Cupressus

Elaeagnus

Escallonia

Euonymus

Fagus

Hedera

Juniperus

Ilex

Laburnum

Laurus

Lavandula

feathery foliage in drooping sprays that can be trimmed to form tall hedges up to 3–3.5m (10–12ft) high.

Plant 45–60cm (18–24in) tall pot-grown specimens 45–60cm (18–24in) apart in autumn or spring, staking each with a cane until fully established to avoid disturbance by wind. Do not prune the growing tip until nearly full height, but shorten any long side shoots with secateurs (hand pruners). Trim mature hedges two or three times a year during summer.

Propagate from semi-ripe cuttings struck in autumn in a closed frame or greenhouse. Mist and rooting hormone powder can assist the rather slow rooting.

CUPRESSUS (CYPRESS)

A large group of evergreen conifers of variable hardiness; none can be said to be very tough, and frost damage is common except in mild areas especially on coasts. They will tolerate a wide range of soils, but grow best in light dry ground which helps to make their foliage denser.

C. glabra (syn. *arizonica*) (smooth Arizona cypress) (7) — a compact conical tree with grey-green foliage, best in the form 'Pyramidalis' whose blue-grey foliage is extremely dense. Useful as a formal clipped specimen tree, or to make a hedge up to 3m (10ft) high. The hardiest species.

C. macrocarpa (Monterey cypress) (8) — once widely planted for hedges because of its fast growth: 60–90cm (2–3ft) a year in good soils. However, it is not very hardy and hedges often develop brown patches in colder inland areas, with entire trees sometimes dying. The species has bright green foliage when young, darkening with age. In favoured districts useful for hedges up to 4.5m (15ft) high. *C.m.* 'Lutea' is a pale gold form; *C.m.* 'Donard Gold' has a richer golden colour; both are best grown in full sun otherwise they tend to turn green.

C. sempervirens (Italian or Mediterranean cypress) (8) — the classic species for formal architectural topiary, unfortunately tender, especially when young, in areas colder than its native climate. The tall slender trees have dense dark-green foliage.

For hedging, plant in spring pot-grown specimens 45–60cm (18–24in) tall and the same distance apart. Protect young plants from frost and wind for the first two or three years. Trim in late spring with shears or preferably secateurs (hand pruners), taking great care not to cut back into old wood which cypress resents.

Propagate as for × *Cupressocyparis*, and by seed sown in pans indoors in spring; transplant to individual small pots when large enough to handle.

ELAEAGNUS

A family of very tough deciduous and evergreen shrubs, mostly fast growing and very responsive to clipping. With their hardy constitution they make excellent hedges and wind-breaks, tolerating most situations including shady and coastal sites, and all soils except shallow chalk. Small but fragrant silvery flowers like those of fuchsias in summer or autumn.

E. angustifolia (oleaster or Russian olive) (2) — a large spiny deciduous tree with silver-grey willowy leaves. Oval golden fruits in autumn. The conspicuous gnarled trunk and shredded bark make this an ideal subject for 'cloud' pruning (see p.83).

E. × *ebbingei* (6) — tall, fast growing evergreen with large silvery leaves. Very hardy and suitable as a hedge up to 180cm (6ft) high.

E. macrophylla (5) — sturdy spreading evergreen, with broad silvery leaves turning shiny green later in the season. Flowers like scented silver bells in autumn. Another subject for 'cloud' pruning, or for training as espaliers.

E. pungens (silverberry or thorny elaeagnus) (6) — vigorous evergreen shrub with some spines; ivory-white fragrant flowers in autumn. Excellent for hedges up to 180–240cm (6–8ft), especially in the forms *E.p.* 'Dicksonii', with erect growth and leaves irregularly margined with deep yellow; 'Maculata' whose leaves have gold patches in their centres; and 'Variegata', with thin pale-yellow edges to the leaves.

Plant bushy pot-grown specimens in autumn or late spring about 45–60cm (18–24in) apart. Trim in early summer

and thereafter if necessary to keep hedges neat. Take care to cut out at an early stage any reverted green shoots of variegated cultivars.

Propagate by semi-ripe cuttings in a greenhouse in autumn; layering in spring; or seeds in a cold frame.

ESCALLONIA

Evergreen or semi-deciduous shrubs with small dark-green leaves, their chief virtue as hedges and wind-breaks being their resilience to salt winds in coastal gardens. Inland many species and cultivars are tender to frost, especially while young. Most will tolerate drought and chalky soils, but are happiest in sandy well-drained soils that are not too rich. Use as semi-formal hedges or trained as espaliers against the shelter of a warm wall.

The species are not as widely available as a number of the cultivars developed (7–8). These include:
E. 'Apple Blossom' — pink and white flowers; slow growing up to 180cm (6ft).
E. 'C.F. Ball' — leaves larger than most and rich crimson tubular flowers; vigorous to 250cm (8ft).
E. 'Donard Seedling' — pink flowers opening to white; vigorous to 250cm (8ft).
E. 'Edinensis' — bright pink flowers; tidy compact bush to 180cm (6ft).
E. 'Ingramii' — large leaves, deep pink flowers; to 250cm (8ft).
E. 'Langleyensis' — rose-pink flowers; graceful arching growth to 270cm–3m (9–10ft).

E. rubra (8) — large glossy leaves and crimson flowers; a robust species for hedging in windy coastal gardens, up to 3m (10ft).

E. rubra var. *macrantha* (syn. *punctata*) (8) — large shiny aromatic leaves with bright rose-pink flowers; sturdy variety for withstanding sea winds; up to 3m (10ft).

Plant pot-grown specimens, 45cm (18in) tall, in autumn or spring 45–60cm (12–18in) apart, or singly for training as espaliers. Trim immediately after flowering, if necessary hard pruning to shape at the same time. As plants flower in late summer or early autumn at the tips of new growth, it is difficult to clip hedges very formally without sacrificing the flowers. If extension growth after pruning is too long, this can be shortened by two-thirds no later than early summer to allow flowering laterals to develop.

Propagate by semi-ripe cuttings in a cold frame in late summer or early autumn; layering in autumn; suckers dug up and replanted in spring.

EUONYMUS (SPINDLE TREE)

A widely varied genus of deciduous and evergreen shrubs, all characterized by adaptability to most soils, especially chalk. The most useful for hedging and training as espaliers are:

E. fortunei (4) — a vigorous hardy trailing or climbing evergreen, with oval clearly veined green leaves, which can be trained to a great height and shaped like ivy on walls. The stems cling by aerial roots in the same way as ivy, though trellis or wires may be used for additional support.

E. japonicus (Japanese spindle tree) (7) — an evergreen shrub with shiny dark-green leaves, a little tender inland but hardy in mild coastal regions where it is popular for hedging and wind-breaks up to 3–3.5m (10–12ft). Where not subject to hard frosts it is very tolerant of urban and industrial atmospheres, and indifferent to most kinds of soil. E.j. 'Macrophyllus Albus' has leaves with broad white margins, while E.j. 'Ovatus Aureus' has golden variegated foliage. Both coloured forms are less vigorous than the species and produce hedges up to 180cm (6ft) high.

Choose container-grown plants about 45cm (18in) tall, and for hedging plant them 45–60cm (18–24in) apart in autumn or spring. Trim at any time with shears; any hard cutting to shape can be done in spring.

Propagate by semi-ripe cuttings in late summer or early autumn in a cold frame.

FAGUS (BEECH)

Fagus sylvatica (common or European beech) (5) is one of the best hardy deciduous hedging plants, thriving in all but heavy waterlogged soils. The oval, pointed leaves, wavy-edged and blunt-toothed, are bright acid-green in spring, becoming darker later and then turning in autumn to a rich golden brown. These dead leaves are retained on young growth until late the following spring, and since hedge-clipping produces a constant supply of new growth, this winter colour is a feature of beech hedges. Very tall and narrow formal hedges up to 6m (20ft) and more in height can be trained with regular clipping, which encourages a dense face of close twiggy growth.

F.s. forma purpurea, (purple or copper beech) is equally suitable for hedging either on its own or combined with green beech.

Plant between autumn and spring young specimens 45–90cm (18in–3ft) tall, spacing them 45–60cm (18–24in) apart. Leave untrimmed for two years to establish, only shortening excessively long side shoots by half. Thereafter clip to shape once or twice during the summer.

Propagate the species from freshly gathered beech nuts (mast) sown outdoors in the autumn and transplanted at two years old. (Varieties are grafted on seedling plants.)

HEDERA (IVY)

A small genus of more-or-less hardy evergreen climbing and trailing plants, containing a large variety of cultivated forms with leaves of different colours and shapes. Ivy will flourish where little else can grow, including dry, heavily shaded and industrial sites, but it is chiefly used as a self-clinging climber, covering large areas of wall with a dense network of stems and leaves that can be shaped into pictorial designs. Ivy can also be trained around formers into complex topiary pieces.

H. helix (common or English ivy) (4) is one of the most useful and reliable species with dark green three- to five-lobed leaves. Once the stems reach the top of a wall or tree they branch out and produce yellow-green flowers in autumn, later bearing black berries in clusters. The stems of this mature 'tree ivy' stage are stout and woody, and bear unlobed leaves. Many cuttings taken in late summer from these adult stems tend to retain these characteristics and grow into self-supporting bushes which can be planted about 45cm (18in) apart to form an attractive hedge.

Numerous forms have been named, including variegated ones with white, gold or purple markings. Though all are worth growing, some of the best include:
H.h. 'Buttercup' — perhaps the best golden form.
H.h. 'Chicago' — smaller, lighter-green leaves than the species.
H.h. 'Hibernica' or 'Irish Ivy' — extremely fast growing and vigorous, with large dark-green leaves.
H.h 'Tricolor' (syn. 'Elegantissima') — triangular leaves with broad creamy-white edges usually tinged with pink.

Always plant pot-grown plants between autumn and spring, laying the long shoots horizontally along the ground to root if rapid coverage of a large area is needed. Trim annually to shape in spring and again during the season whenever necessary.

Propagate by firm cuttings in early autumn in the open ground or by rooted layers. 'Tree ivy' can either be grown on its own roots or grafted on to common or English ivy root stocks.

ILEX (HOLLY)

One of the classic topiary and hedging plants. Those mentioned below are all hardy evergreens, flourishing in any good soil and tolerating both shady sites and urban and industrial pollution; variegated kinds display the best colours when grown in full sun. Although leaf loss can occur with extreme exposure, many species and cultivars are very wind-resistant. When clipped as a hedge holly makes an impenetrable barrier, all the more effective because of the prickly leaves borne by most kinds, although this does mean care must be taken when weeding beneath the plants. Foliage is produced right down to ground level when the plants are severely clipped, but few berries will be borne; where these are wanted hedges must be grown informally, and both male and female plants should grow in close proximity. Holly makes a handsome background of solid rich colour when grown on its own, but it is equally useful for mixing in a tapestry hedge with other species both evergreen and deciduous.

Ilex × altaclarensis (Highclere holly) **(7)** — a group of very vigorous broad-leaved shrubs, most of which are ideally suited for hedging up to 3–3.5m (10–12ft).
I. × a. 'Camelliifolia' — purple stems and large, often spineless dark-green leaves which are an attractive shade of deep red when young. Female.
I. × a. 'Golden King' — broad, virtually unarmed leaves brightly edged yellow. Female.
I. × a. 'Hodginsii' — vigorous, purple-stemmed with large and distinctly shiny leaves with variable spines. Male.

Ilex aquifolium (common or English holly) **(7)** — possibly the very best and toughest species for hedges up to 5.5–6m (18–20ft) high. Numerous different cultivars exist, some of the most attractive being:
I.a. 'Argentea Marginata' (broad-leaved silver holly) — with clear white edges to the leaves. Both male and, more commonly, female.
I.a. 'Ferox' (hedgehog holly) — slower growing form with smaller leaves, each fiercely armed on the upper surface with short congested spines. Makes an excellent barrier hedge. Male. There are silver and gold variegated forms.
I.a. 'Golden Queen' — spiny, dark-green leaves with paler markings and a clear golden edge. Young stems sometimes red. Male.

Ilex cornuta (Chinese or horned holly) **(7)** — a compact slow growing species with squarish leaves, each corner with a sharp spine. The cultivar 'Burfordii', whose shiny deep-green leaves have a terminal spine only, makes a dense dwarf hedge. Up to 240cm (8ft).

Ilex crenata (Japanese holly) **(6–7)** —a dwarf, slow growing holly, with tiny shiny leaves, ideal for a low dense hedge. To 180cm (6ft).

Ilex glabra (inkberry or winterberry) **(5)** — a slow growing dense bush with small leaves, shiny and smooth. Not happy on chalky soils, but elsewhere slowly spreads by means of underground stolons. To 180cm (6ft).

Choose plants 45–90cm (18in–3ft) tall, either container-grown or root-balled; make sure larger specimens have been transplanted at the nursery at least once. Plant in early autumn or late spring, 45cm (18in) apart for short hollies, 60–75cm (24–30in) for taller kinds. (Loss of some of the oldest leaves the spring or summer after planting is often a sign that a bush is rooting healthily.) In colder areas protect young plants from winds until well established. Prune large-leaved forms with secateurs (hand pruners) in spring or late summer, smaller kinds with shears.

Propagate from seed, which takes at least a year to germinate; from semi-ripe cuttings in a cold frame in late summer or autumn; budding ornamental varieties as standard trees on common holly root stocks.

JUNIPERUS (JUNIPER)

Although most usually grown these days as named cultivars for decorative specimen shrubs, many junipers respond very well to trimming as hedges, and in the eighteenth century were often clipped into arbours and other simple topiary shapes.

J. communis (common juniper) **(3)** — the species traditionally most commonly used, tough, hardy and wind-resistant, fairly slow growing and happy on most soils, especially chalk. The erect slender form *J.c.* 'Hibernica' (Irish juniper) has blue-grey feathery foliage and makes a slim formal hedge 180cm–3m (6–10ft) high; upright growths may require tying in to the main stems when forced out of line by wind or the weight of snow.

Juniperus sabina (savin) **(3)** — a low, spreading species with dark-green foliage and stiff arching growth. When crushed or cut it has a pungent smell. In the past it was commonly clipped into low hedges up to about 90cm (3ft) high.

Plant pot-grown specimens 45–60cm (18–24in) tall, spaced 45cm (18in) apart in autumn or spring. Clip during the summer as necessary.
Propagate by sowing seeds in March (germination may take a year or more), or from semi-ripe cuttings in a cold frame in autumn.

LABURNUM

Hardy deciduous flowering trees, usually grown freely as garden trees, but also ideally suited to training on wires or trellis as espaliers or over a framework as a tunnel. The best cultivar for this is *L. × watereri* 'Vossii' **(5)** with glossy trifoliate leaves and very long racemes of golden-yellow blooms in May and June.

Plant young trees about 180cm (6ft) high between autumn and spring, spacing them 180–240cm (6–8ft) apart if they are to be grown over a tunnel frame. While young prune after flowering to encourage a network of strong stems and tie these in to the wires or frame. Once the main branches are established on an espalier, cut side shoots after flowering to one or two buds beyond the base of the previous year's growth to maintain short flowering spurs. On tunnels weave and tie in long shoots to form a dense canopy of stems, reaching through the roof to cut off any growth projecting above the tunnel and similarly facing up the sides.
Propagate by hard-wood cuttings outdoors in late autumn; grafting on to common broom *(Cytisus)* seedlings; seed in spring.

LAURUS

L. nobilis (sweet bay or bay laurel) **(7)** is a popular evergreen Mediterranean tree with glossy aromatic leaves often dried for culinary use. Its natural habit is broadly conical, but the dense foliage is easily pruned to shape as a hedge up to about 6m (20ft) high, and as ball-shaped standard trees in the open ground or tubs. Unfortunately it is not reliably hardy when young, and even mature trees have been damaged in patches or down to ground level by severe frost, or occasionally killed outright. The form *L.n. forma angustifolia* (willow-leaf bay) with long slender light-green leaves, seems to be much hardier than the species.

Bay laurel will grow in any soil that is well-drained and moderately fertile. Plant pot-grown specimens 30–45cm (12–18in) tall, spaced 60cm (2ft) apart for hedges, in spring and protect from cold winds for the first few years.

Ligustrum

Myrtus

Lonicera

Osmanthus

Paliurus

Phillyrea

Photinia

Picca

Pinus

Pittosporum

Platanus

Prunus

Trim to shape with secateurs (hand pruners) once or twice as necessary during summer.

Propagate from semi-ripe cuttings in late summer or early autumn in a cold frame. (Ensure that this is frost-free in colder areas.)

LAVANDULA (LAVENDER)

Evergreen bushy fragrant herbs, very popular in gardens for dwarf hedging, but often allowed to become leggy and misshapen from neglect. As plants are usually grown for their sweet-scented mauve or purple flowers in summer, as well as for the grey-green aromatic foliage, it is difficult to keep hedges strictly formal; but with two or three well-timed trims each year it is possible to have both flowers and tidy plants. Lavender prefers a sunlit position on well-drained soil that is light and contains lime.

L. angustifolia (syn. *spica*) (old English lavender) (5) — a group of vigorous types of lavender, all of them attractive, hardy and reliable:
L.a. 'Grappenhall' — robust and taller than most, making a sturdy hedge up to 90cm (3ft). Very fragrant lavender-blue flowers in July.
L.a. 'Hidcote' (syn. 'Nana Atropurpurea') — compact dense growth for hedges up to 60cm (2ft). Thick spikes of violet flowers in early July.

L. stoechas (French lavender) (8) — very aromatic foliage and flowers, dense dwarf growth ideal for hedging 35–45cm (15–18in) high. Much less hardy than English lavender, but reliable once established in a sunny sheltered site. Deep purple, strongly scented flowers in July.

Plant one-year old specimens in spring in rich soil, spacing tall varieties 30cm (12in) apart, dwarf ones 20cm (9in). Water the plants in and keep the soil moist during the first summer with a mulch. Clip hedges with shears in spring and again immediately after flowering, cutting to or just below the outline of the hedge to encourage bushy growth and to prevent bare patches from developing lower down.

Propagate lavender by layering, or from cuttings in a cold frame in late summer.

LIGUSTRUM (PRIVET)

Vigorous hardy shrubs, indifferent to soil and aspect. Some species are deciduous, others semi-evergreen or evergreen in milder climatic zones. Privet has earned itself a bad name, partly owing to former over-planting but also because the roots tend to extract every particle of nutrient from the surrounding soil, to the detriment of neighbouring plants. If the roots are cut back within bounds with a spade, and the hedge is fed with a mulch annually, there will be little cause for complaint. Plants stand very frequent clipping and can be shaped as hedges or into large figurative topiary.

L. delavayanum (8) — small, glossy evergreen leaves; dense panicles of white flowers. Good for hedges up to 180cm (6ft) or as standard clipped trees. Not as hardy as some species.

L. japonicum (Japanese privet) (7) — very dense habit, large glossy evergreen leaves and heavy heads of creamy-white flowers. For medium-sized standards or hedges up to 180cm (6ft).

L. lucidum (waxleaf privet) (8) — long shiny evergreen leaves and very handsome heads of bloom in late summer. An excellent species for clipping as a specimen tree to reveal its attractive bark, trained to a height of around 3m (10ft) though it will grow much higher. Outstanding variegated forms exist, most notably *L.l.* 'Excelsum Superbum', less vigorous than the species, with yellow or cream edges and splashes on its leaves.

L. ovalifolium (oval-leaved, common Japanese, or California privet) (6) — a large tree when left unpruned, but best known as the species most commonly used for hedging up to about 3m (10ft). Plain and robust.
L.o. 'Aureum' (golden privet) — a very attractive brightly variegated form whether grown as a specimen or clipped as topiary or hedging up to 180cm (6ft). Full sunlight encourages the best colour, as does frequent trimming, because the youngest growth is the most golden, a green central band developing on each leaf as it matures.

Plant 30–45cm (12–18in) tall specimens 30–45cm (12–18in) apart from autumn to spring, and cut back to

15–20cm (6–9in) high after planting. For standards select a larger bush with a strong leading shoot and secure this to a strong cane. Continue to tie in further growth, while cutting off lowest shoots each year as more develop at the top, until the full height is reached, when the leader can be stopped and a branching head of foliage allowed to form. Trim hedges several times in summer, cutting out cleanly any green shoots that appear on variegated plants. Hard prune overgrown hedges to shape in April.

Propagate by soft cuttings in a cold frame in summer, or semi-ripe cuttings outdoors in autumn.

LONICERA (HONEYSUCKLE)

Many of the shrubby honeysuckles make excellent informal hedges, but two species in particular can be closely trimmed to form hedges of neat foliage or small specimens of topiary. Neither of these is as fragrant in flower as more commonly grown honeysuckles.

L. nitida (boxleaf honeysuckle) (7) — a dense evergreen with tiny leaves shaped like those of box. Very fast growing and easily clipped or shaped. A little more sensitive to frost than privet, and tends to become bare at the base unless regularly tended. The form usually supplied under this name is in fact *L.n.* 'Ernest Wilson'. The variants 'Fertilis' (sometimes known as *L. ligustrina*) and 'Yunnan' are both similar to the species but their growth is more erect and robust. *L.n.* 'Baggesen's Gold', a fine rich yellow form, is equally suitable for topiary or hedging up to 120cm (4ft).

L. pileata (privet honeysuckle) (6) — a dwarf widely spreading shrub with bright-green narrowly oval leaves, turning darker as they age. Hedge to 90cm (3ft).

Plant 30–45cm (12–18in) tall specimens 30cm (12in) apart for hedges in spring and cut back to half their height after planting. Shape a pronounced batter to hedges to keep the base well clothed. Thriving plants may need clipping as often as privet during the summer. Hard prune overgrown plants in April.

Propagate by layering in autumn or by semi-hardwood cuttings in a shady frame in late summer or hard-wood cuttings outside or in a frame in autumn.

MYRTUS (MYRTLE)

Evergreen shrubs hardy only in warm well-drained soils in mild and coastal regions, where they make easily cultivated and maintained hedges, either clipped formally or pruned just once annually and allowed to flower and fruit. The thick dark shiny green leaves are aromatic and produce a dense face when regularly trimmed. Simple formal topiary can also be shaped with shears. Two species are commonly used:

M. communis (common myrtle) (9) — fragrant small glossy leaves. Will reach 3m (10ft) or more against a warm wall, but as a hedge is best kept to about 180cm (6ft). White flowers in summer, followed by black berries.

M. ugni (syn. *Eugenia ugni*, *Ugni molinae*) (Chilean guava) (9) — slow growing evergreen with oval leathery leaves. Hedge to 120cm (4ft). Rosy-white bell-shaped flowers and edible red berries.

Plant in spring, spacing 45cm (18in) tall pot-grown specimens 60cm (2ft) apart for hedges. Trim in spring, and again when necessary if a neat finish is required.

Propagate by semi-ripe cuttings in summer in a greenhouse.

OSMANTHUS

Hardy and half-hardy evergreen shrubs, a few of which stand clipping into hedges or training as espaliers against a wall.

O. × *burkwoodii* (formerly *Osmarea* × *burkwoodii*) (7) — a hybrid between *O. delavayi* and *O. decorus*; a hardy evergreen with dark shiny leaves with serrated edges, and fragrant small white flowers in spring. Growth is slow and compact, for hedges up to 250cm (8ft). Hardy and happy in any good soil, including chalk.

O. decora (formerly *Phillyrea decora*) (6) — a very tough evergreen species, often wider than tall, with large leathery leaves, glossy green; fragrant white

flowers in late spring. Hedges to 180cm (6ft). Best pruned with secateurs (hand pruners) to avoid cutting the large leaves.

O. delavayi (7) — small glossy dark-green leaves and tiny sweet-scented white flowers in spring. Hardy except in very severe winters, and slow growing in colder areas. Espaliers can be trained against walls to 3m (10ft) high, but hedges should be kept to about 120cm (4ft).

O. heterophyllus (holly osmanthus) (7) — dense shrub with shiny dark green holly-like leaves, often spiny, and fragrant flowers in autumn. Makes an excellent slow growing hedge to 3m (10ft). There are several coloured forms, including 'Aureomarginatus' whose leaves have deep yellow edges; 'Latifolius Variegatus', a broad-leaved form with silver variegations; and 'Purpureus' with purple young growth.

Plant 30–45cm (12–18in) tall specimens in spring, 45–60cm (18–24in) apart in well-drained soil with plenty of humus. Prune to shape in late spring. Trim hedges thereafter when necessary and depending whether flowers are wanted. Wall-trained plants can be pruned after flowering, subsequent long stems being cut back to side shoots at any time.

Propagate by semi-ripe cuttings in late summer or early autumn in a cold frame or greenhouse.

OSMAREA

See *Osmanthus* × *burkwoodii*.

PALIURUS

Deciduous trees and shrubs, one of which, *P. spina-christi* (Christ's thorn), (7) was recorded by Loudon as used for hedging in Italian gardens. Best grown in mild areas in freely draining soils where it will make a dense, extremely spiny hedge up to 180cm (6ft) high. Plants bear small yellow flowers in late summer, and their oval leaves turn a bright gold in the autumn.

Plant in autumn small bushy specimens about 45cm (18in) apart. Clip in early summer and again later on if

straggling stems extend too far beyond the hedge; alternatively, weave them into the face of the hedge.

Propagate by layers or suckers in autumn, or by root cuttings in a cold frame or greenhouse during winter.

PHILLYREA

Handsome hardy evergreen flowering shrubs, closely related to osmanthus, with narrow shiny dark green leaves and fragrant white flowers in late spring and summer. They have a long history of use as hedges and topiary: Loudon wrote that plants were often clipped into 'figures of balls, men, animals etc.' They are happy in most soils and aspects.

P. angustifolia (7) — very dense habit, especially when clipped regularly; early-summer flowering. The form 'rosmarinifolia' is very compact and tidy in growth, with narrower leaves. Hedge or topiary up to 240cm (8ft) but fairly slow growing.

For hedges, use young plants 45cm (18in) tall, planted 45–60cm (18–24in) apart in autumn or spring. Trim after flowering and again when necessary.

Propagate by semi-ripe cuttings in a cold frame in autumn or layering in spring.

PHOTINIA

Evergreen members of this Asiatic group make excellent hedging subjects in milder areas; elsewhere they tend to be sensitive to frost, and seldom flower or fruit. The shiny leaves are often red or bronze when they first appear, later turning dark green. Unlike deciduous species, evergreen photinias are lime-tolerant.

P. × *fraseri* (8) — large vigorous shrub with copper-coloured young foliage. Only fully hardy in milder districts. The form 'Red Robin' has brilliant red young growth, but 'Robusta' with less vivid colouring seems to be hardier than either of these. Hedge to 180cm (6ft) or more.

P. glabra (Japanese photinia) (8) — hardier, medium-sized shrub, with dark-green leathery leaves and bronze young growth. The early growth on the form 'Rubens' is a much brighter red. Hedge to 180cm (6ft).

P. serrulata (Chinese photinia) **(7)** — a large vigorous species, much hardier than *P. × fraseri*. Deeply serrated leaves bronze-red in youth. Hedge to 3m (10ft).

Plant bushy pot-grown plants in spring 60cm (24in) apart in light, well-drained soil. Encourage young branching growth by pinching out growing tips regularly as the hedge develops; once fully established two or three trims from late spring onwards should be enough to maintain a neat shape. Flowering and fruiting minimal or not at all when clipped.

Propagate by layers in autumn; by semi-ripe cuttings in a greenhouse in late summer; by seed when ripe or in spring in a cold frame.

PICEA (SPRUCE)

Hardy evergreen conifers, often planted to make tall screens but with regular clipping several species are suitable for hedges in smaller gardens or for architectural topiary as depicted in seventeenth-century Dutch paintings. Spruces are happier on moist deep soils, although once established they will tolerate drier or poor soils.

P. abies (Norway spruce) **(3)** — hardy tapering species with short dark green needles. Hedge to 4.5–6m (15–20ft).

P. glauca (white spruce) **(3)** — extremely hardy, with grey-green foliage, otherwise similar to *P. abies*. The cultivar 'Conica' is slow growing, very dense and compact, with very bright green needles, ideal for dwarf hedges to about 90m (3ft).

P. omorika (Serbian spruce) **(4)** — hardy and adaptable, tolerating urban pollution and poor soils. Graceful habit with dark green needles, greyish beneath. Up to 3–4.5m (10–15ft).

Plant in autumn or late spring young specimens that have been transplanted once, spacing them 60–90cm (2–3ft) apart. Do not allow to dry out during the first two or three years, and be prepared to shelter them from cold winds until established. Trim in spring, removing any vigorous protruding

branches deep within the plants and then facing up hedges with shears, repeating this superficial clip in summer if necessary.

Propagate by seeds sown outdoors in spring.

PINUS (PINE)

Although often planted as such, pines are not a suitable medium for screens and wind-breaks because of the tendency for them to lose their lower branches. One or two species, however, make handsome subjects for 'cloud' pruning (see p.83), particularly *Pinus parviflora* (Japanese white pine) **(6)**, the tree pictured on the familiar 'Willow Pattern' china. The foliage is a rich blue-green, while the trunk and widely spreading branches have a dark purple bark that flakes off in patches. It is very hardy and grows well in all types of well-drained soil.

Plant young specimens 30–45cm (12–18in) tall in autumn or spring, spacing them not less than 60cm (2ft) apart, using pot-grown plants to avoid root disturbance.

Propagate by seeds sown outdoors in spring.

PITTOSPORUM

Evergreen trees of doubtful hardiness, although they make very attractive hedges in mild and coastal areas. Most sites are suitable provided they are well-drained and not very shaded.

P. crassifolium (karo) **(10)** — one of the hardiest species in coastal districts, with oval dark-green leaves, white-felted beneath. Forms a dense hedge up to 3m (10ft) in favoured areas where it may also bear deep purple flowers in late spring.

P. tenuifolium (tawhiwhi, kohuhu) **(8)** — also relatively hardy with bright pale-green leaves on black stems, popular with florists. Deep purple sweet-scented flowers appear in spring. Hedge to 3m (12ft).

Small young pot-grown plants are best, no more than 60cm (2ft) tall. Plant them 45cm (18in) apart in spring and provide shelter from cold winds until established.

Propagate by semi-ripe cuttings in summer in a greenhouse propagator or closed cold frame, or by seeds in warmth in spring.

PLATANUS (PLANE)

P. × hispanica (syn. *× acerifolia*) (London plane), with large palmate leaves and attractively mottled bark, is a popular subject for pollarding and pleaching up to about 5m (16ft) high. This hybrid, fast growing and hardy, is noted for its tolerance of all kinds of moist soils and urban pollution.

For pleaching, plant young trees between autumn and spring 180cm–3m (6–10ft) apart and shorten all growth by half. In succeeding years, thin side shoots and lower branches until a clear stem and evenly placed series of branches is established for training sideways on wires or a timber or metal frame.

Propagate in spring by hardwood cuttings in a cold frame.

PRUNUS

A large group of hardy shrubs and trees, most of them deciduous. Although normally grown for their flowers and fruit, several are excellent for hedging, growing in most soils that are not too acid.

P. cerasifera (myrobalan or cherry plum) — a deciduous spiny tree with crowded white blossom in spring and small red plums in summer on plants that are not formally trimmed. Very dense twiggy growth when clipped, and makes a valuable hedge up to 180cm (6ft), especially on clay soils. Excellent subject for plashing (see p.73). The forms 'Nigra', with deep purple leaves and stems, and 'Pissardii', whose rich red young foliage turns purple later, are both fine alternatives for hedging. Up to 180cm (6ft). Plant 60–90cm (2–3ft) tall specimens in autumn or winter 60cm (2ft) apart and cut back to 30cm (12in). Trim after flowering and again in summer.

P. incisa (Fuji cherry) — medium-sized shrub with small leaves that assume brilliant colours in autumn, and masses of pinkish white flowers in early spring. Can be trimmed very

Pyracantha

Ribes

Rhamnus

Rosmarinus

Santolina

Ruta

Sarcococca

Taxus

Thuja

Teucrium

Tilia

Tsuga

neatly as a hedge up to 180cm (6ft). Plant 45cm (18in) apart in autumn and winter. Prune as for myrobalan.

P. lusitanica (Portugal or bay laurel) — hardy evergreen tree with shiny dark-green leaves and long racemes of scented white flowers in summer. Makes an excellent dense hedge up to 3.5–4.5m (12–15ft) tall, provided it is pruned regularly to avoid gaps occurring. Choose plants 60cm (2ft) tall and space them 60cm (2ft) apart in autumn or spring. Trim with secateurs (hand pruners) in spring and summer. Maintain a gentle batter on tall hedges. The form 'Myrtifolia' is very dense and slow growing, with smaller leaves than the type, and can be used for formal standards where bay laurel is too tender.

Propagate by hard-wood cuttings in a cold frame in autumn.

PYRACANTHA (FIRETHORN)

Hardy evergreen thorny shrubs, usually grown for their white flowers in early summer and brightly coloured berries which often hang all winter. These can be seen to advantage when plants are trained as espaliers on walls, where some species reach 3.5–4.5m (12–15ft) or more, but several kinds also make valuable foliage plants for formal hedges, in which case few fruits will be borne. Pyracanthas flourish in most situations and any fertile soil.

P. atalantioides (7) — large, upright robust shrub with dark-green glossy leaves and bright scarlet berries. Excellent for walls, when it will reach 4.5m (15ft), or for hedges up to 240cm (8ft). The similar form 'Aurea' has bright yellow fruits.

P. coccinea (7) — tall vigorous species with oval, toothed leaves. Best in the form 'Lalandei' which is more erect with large dense clusters of deep orange berries. To 4.5m (15ft) on a wall or 180cm (6ft) as a hedge.

P. rogersiana (6) — large shrub with small pointed leaves and heavy clusters of red-orange berries. The form 'Flava' has yellow fruits. To 3m (10ft) on walls, 180cm (6ft) as hedges.

Pot-grown plants are best, about 60cm (2ft) high and planted in autumn

or spring 60cm (2ft) apart for hedges. Summer-prune new growth on espalier side shoots to half their length, shortening them again to two or three leaves in winter. Hedges grown for their impenetrable foliage can be clipped to shape any time from spring onwards; if fruits are required, shorten growth back with secateurs (hand pruners) to suitably placed clusters of juvenile berries after flowering and keep young shoots clipped to this point.

Propagate by semi-ripe cuttings in late summer in a greenhouse; seeds when ripe or in spring in a cold frame.

RHAMNUS (BUCKTHORN)

A large genus of deciduous and evergreen trees and shrubs, one of which, *R. alaternus* (Italian buckthorn) (7), was widely grown in the seventeenth century as a handsome evergreen hedge that could be shaped with shears in the same way as holly. It is a large bushy shrub, fast growing with small dark shiny green leaves, and pale green flowers in spring followed by black fruits; makes a hedge up to 3m (10ft). Most soils and aspects are suitable, and plants will tolerate urban pollution, but they are not fully hardy in cold inland areas. The coloured form 'Argenteovariegata' with leaves marbled and edged in creamy-grey is very attractive but a little more tender.

Plant small pot-grown bushy plants 60cm (2ft) apart. Clip several times during the growing season to keep hedges neat and prevent loose growth.

Propagate in autumn by layering or by hard-wood cuttings outdoors.

RIBES (CURRANT)

Two deciduous members of this genus are valuable subjects for wall training or for hedging. Both are indifferent to soil type.

R. speciosum (fuchsia-flowered gooseberry) (7) — a deciduous or semi-evergreen shrub which in cold areas prefers to be grown against a wall for protection, where it will reach 3m (10ft). There it can be trained like a fruit espalier to enhance the pendulous

clusters of slender bright red fuchsia-like flowers in late spring. Red bristly stems bear shiny green foliage resembling that of a gooseberry.

Plant pot-grown specimens in spring, and train a simple framework of stems against wires or trellis. Trim to shape after flowering, and during summer shorten by half any long side shoots that threaten to crowd others. Propagate by semi-ripe cuttings in a cold frame in late summer.

R. uva-crispa (syn. *grossularia*) (gooseberry) (3) — spiny shrubs with bright green three-lobed leaves. For hedging a vigorous erect variety should be chosen, such as 'Early Sulphur', 'May Duke' or 'Whitesmith'. Reduced but still useful crops of fruit will be produced on bushes clipped as hedges, up to 120cm (4ft).

Plant bushy specimens in autumn 30–45cm (12–18in) apart. If there is a pronounced single stem, or 'leg', plant deeply to bury this so that the lowest branches can root and add to the density of the hedge. For pruning and propagation, see p.76.

ROSMARINUS (ROSEMARY)

The common rosemary, *R. officinalis* (8), has been used since classical Roman times for hedging. A dense aromatic hardy evergreen shrub with narrow grey-green leaves and small blue flowers in spring, rosemary will tolerate most freely draining soils although it prefers light soil and a sunny site. The vigorous form 'Fastigiatus', sometimes known as 'Miss Jessop's Variety', is more upright than the species. Hedges up to 120cm (4ft) high.

Plant 45cm (18in) tall specimens the same distance apart in spring. Trim after flowering and again if necessary later in the season, but try to avoid cutting into old wood.

Propagate by semi-ripe cuttings in a cold frame in late summer or early autumn.

RUTA (RUE)

R. graveolens (common rue or herb of grace) (5) makes a very attractive aromatic hedge about 60cm (2ft) high, suitable for edging or internal hedges on any well-drained soil in a sunny position. This medicinal herb has pungent blue-green dissected leaves, to which some people are unfortunately allergic, and in summer small yellow flowers which are best sheared off to keep a tight shape to the hedge. The form 'Jackman's Blue' is bushier and more compact than the type, with rich blue foliage.

Young plants 15–22cm (6–9in) tall should be planted 30cm (12in) apart in spring. Trim with shears any time during the growing season.

Propagate by semi-hardwood cuttings in a shaded frame during late summer or early autumn; *R. graveolens* also by seed outdoors in spring.

SANTOLINA

Evergreen Mediterranean shrubs with aromatic finely-cut foliage. Best for hedging up to about 45cm (18in) tall is *S. chamaecyparissus* (cotton lavender) (6) which has been used for this purpose for centuries. The felted filigree leaves are almost white. Plants are hardy in well-drained soils in full sun, and bear bright yellow button-shaped flowers in summer. *S. neapolitana* is larger in all respects but tends to looser growth when trimmed as a hedge, up to 75cm (30in) high.

Plant young pot-grown stock 15–22cm (6–9in) high about 30cm (12in) apart in spring. Clip in spring and either allow to flower, shearing off the dead heads immediately afterwards, or keep trim with two or three additional cuts during the season.

Propagate from semi-ripe heel cuttings in a cold frame in autumn or from hard-wood cuttings outside a little later.

SARCOCOCCA (SWEET BOX)

A group of small slow-growing evergreen shrubs allied to box. They have small shiny leaves and tiny almond-scented white flowers in late winter, grow happily on any moist soils including chalk, and in full sun or semi-shade.

S. confusa (5) — dense growth of sharply elliptical leaves; cream flowers

and black berries. Reaches 180cm (6ft) eventually.

S. hookerana digyna (5) — relatively hardy with bright narrow green leaves and white flowers followed by black berries. The form 'Purple Stem' is similar, but with a red-purple flush to stems and leaf ribs. Hedge eventually to 120cm (4ft).

Plant pot-grown stock 30cm (12in) apart between autumn and spring. Clip in spring and then as necessary.

Propagate by semi hard-wood cuttings in a cold frame in autumn.

TAXUS (YEW)

Classic topiary and hedging plants. Yews are hardy evergreen conifers, tolerating almost all well-drained soils and sites including shade, and very responsive to clipping and hard pruning. Although reputedly slow growing, young bushes will increase their height by 45cm (18in) a year once in their stride. Male and female flowers are usually borne on separate trees.

T. baccata (common yew, English yew) (6) — has very dark green conifer foliage and bright-red poisonous berries. There are numerous forms, including many with cream or yellow variegation, but although all make attractive specimen trees none is as vigorous as the type. 'Elegantissima' is the best golden yew for topiary or dense hedging. Hedges up to 6m (20ft).

T. cuspidata (Japanese yew) (4) — hardier than *T. baccata* in very cold areas. A spreading shrub rather than a tree, with dark green leaves paler beneath. Hedge to 180cm–3m (6–10ft).

T. × media (4) — a group of hybrids between the two previous species and sharing their qualities. Several very hardy named forms are widely available. The best of these for hedging are 'Brownii', slow growing and tending to become wider than it is tall; 'Hicksii', erect with very deep green foliage; and 'Sargentii', upright in growth and very dense. Hedges to 3–6m (10–20ft), according to cultivar.

Plant small bushy trees up to 90cm (3ft) tall (these will be several years old) 45–60cm (18–24in) apart for hedges in autumn or spring. Prepare

the ground thoroughly with plenty of humus, and mulch after planting. Clip from early summer onwards.

Propagate by seed sown outdoors in spring, or semi-ripe cuttings in a cold frame in autumn. *T. × media* must be raised vegetatively.

TEUCRIUM (GERMANDER)

T. chamaedrys (wall germander) (5) is a valuable aromatic evergreen shrub with a dwarf bushy habit. The erect hairy stems are closely covered with small rich-green toothed leaves, and bear small rose-pink flowers in late summer. Ideal for dwarf hedging up to 30cm (12in) tall, in knot gardens and parterres or to edge herb beds in sunny, well-drained positions. Spreads slowly by means of a creeping root stock.

Plant bushy pot-grown specimens 22cm (9in) apart in autumn or spring. Trim once or twice in summer to keep plants tidy.

Propagate by division in spring; by semi hard-wood cuttings in a cold frame in late summer; by layering in autumn.

THUJA (ARBOR-VITAE)

Hardy evergreen conifers with aromatic foliage which varies from species to species. Several are very valuable hedging plants, producing dense faces with regular clipping and retaining their growth down to ground level. They are best grown in moist well-drained soils. The two most useful species are:

T. occidentalis (American arbor-vitae) (3) — very hardy tree with horizontal branches and dark-green foliage, pale green beneath and turning bronze in winter. Hedges to 3.5–4.5m (12–15ft). The form 'Fastigiata' (syns. 'Pyramidalis', 'Columnaris', 'Stricta') is a narrow columnar tree with dense foliage, a useful substitute for the Mediterranean cypress where the latter is too frost-sensitive.

Plant specimens up to 90cm (3ft) tall, 60cm (2ft) apart in autumn or spring.

T. plicata (syns. *lobbii*, *gigantea*) (giant arbor-vitae, western red cedar)

(5) — a less hardy tree than the preceding species in very cold regions, but a more sympathetic hedging medium. Its dark shiny green foliage makes an excellent background and with regular clipping forms a dense face. Leaves stay green throughout the winter. Hedges up to 4.5m (15ft) or more. 'Zebrina' is an attractive gold form with similar vigour, ideal for shorter hedging up to 3m (10ft).

Plant 45cm (18in) tall specimens 60–90cm (2–3ft) apart in autumn or spring.

Clip the sides of young arbor-vitae hedges during the early years to encourage density, but allow the leader to reach nearly full height before being stopped. Trim from late spring onwards.

Propagate by seed sown outdoors in spring, or by heel cuttings in autumn in a cold frame.

TILIA (LIME, LINDEN)

Hardy deciduous trees that will grow in almost any fertile soil, and tolerate urban and industrial atmospheres. They have been renowned over the centuries for their tolerance of hard pruning and the flexibility of the stems, which has made them a popular subject for pleaching and pollarding. Sweet-scented pale yellow flowers, which are highly attractive to bees, are borne in summer.

T. cordata (small-leaved lime, small-leaved European linden) (4) — a medium-sized tree with smaller leaves than most, heart-shaped and dark green, paler beneath.

T. × euchlora (Crimean linden) (6) — an elegant hybrid which does not suffer so badly from attacks by aphids as some other limes. Glossy leaves and a dense twiggy habit when clipped as a hedge up to 3m (10ft).

T. × europaea (common lime, European linden) (4) — the most widely planted species for street trees, decorative training, and occasionally for hedges up to 3.5m (12ft) or more. A very large vigorous tree with a tendency to sucker from the base.

T. platyphyllos (broad-leaved lime, long-leaved linden) (4) — a vigorous tree with very large dark-green leaves, covered in down. The form 'Rubra' has very attractive deep-red young shoots that are particularly conspicuous in winter.

Plant young trees, with stakes, between autumn and spring 240cm–3.5m (8–12ft) apart depending on their proposed use. Prune after leaf fall, and train in young shoots as they grow.

Propagate by seeds sown outdoors in spring; suckers dug up in autumn; by layering in spring or summer.

TSUGA (HEMLOCK)

Elegant evergreen conifers, with fine foliage easily clipped into dense hedges up to 6m (20ft) or more. They grow best on moist well-drained soils.

T. canadensis (eastern hemlock) (3) — the best species for chalky soils, very hardy and thriving in areas of high rainfall. The undersides of the green leaves are marked by two pale bands which give the foliage a silvery appearance.

T. heterophylla (western hemlock) (3) — a large vigorous tree with dark-green foliage, paler beneath, on branches that arch gracefully upwards. Tolerates shade.

Plant young trees 45cm (18in) tall in autumn 60cm (2ft) apart. Trim as for thuja. Established hedges will need clipping two or three times during the growing season.

Propagate by seeds sown outdoors in spring or by semi-ripe cuttings in a cold frame in late summer or autumn.

GARDENS TO VISIT

Below is a brief selection of British and American gardens which contain fine or unusual examples of topiary, clipped hedges and parterres.

BRITAIN

Ascott Gardens, Wing, Buckinghamshire
(topiary sundial)

Barnsley House, near Cirencester, Gloucestershire
(hedges and knot garden)

Chatsworth House, Chatsworth, Derbyshire
(stilt and serpentine hedges)

Crathes Castle, Kincardine, Grampian *(yew hedges)*

Elvaston Castle Country Park, near Derby
(large topiary garden)

Great Dixter, Northiam, East Sussex
(topiary garden and hedges)

Haseley Court, Little Haseley, Oxfordshire
(topiary chess set)

Hatfield House, Hatfield, Hertfordshire *(knot garden)*

Hidcote Manor, near Chipping Campden,
Gloucestershire *(yew, pleached and tapestry hedges)*

Knightshayes Court, near Tiverton, Devon
('foxhunt' hedge)

Levens Hall, near Kendal, Cumbria
(eighteenth-century topiary garden)

Mount Ephraim, Hernhill, near Faversham, Kent
(topiary garden)

Mount Stewart, County Down, Northern Ireland
(topiary harp and figures)

Nymans, Handcross, West Sussex *(specimen topiary)*

Packwood House, Hockley Heath, Warwickshire
(topiary 'Sermon on the Mount')

Pitmedden Garden, Gordon, Grampian *(parterre)*

Rockingham Castle, Corby, Northamptonshire
('elephant' yew hedge)

Powis Castle, Welshpool, Powys *(yew hedges)*

Tudor House Museum, Southampton, Hampshire
(knot garden)

USA

Atlanta Botanical Garden, Atlanta, Georgia
(knot garden)

Brooklyn Botanic Garden, Brooklyn, New York
(knot garden)

Dumbarton Oaks, Washington D.C.
(hedges and cypress arbour)

Green Animals Topiary Garden, Portsmouth,
Rhode Island *(topiary figures)*

Walter Hunnewell Arboretum, Wellesley,
Massachusetts *(topiary garden)*

Ladew Topiary Gardens, Monkton, Maryland
*(topiary figures; also the location of a projected reference
library of American topiary)*

Longwood Gardens, Kennett Square, Pennsylvania
(hedges and specimen topiary)

Mount Vernon, Virginia *(box parterre)*

Villa Vizcaya, Miami, Florida
(Renaissance-style parterre)

Williamsburg, Virginia *(parterres and specimen topiary)*

Unusual topiary figures can also be seen at:
Disneyland, Anaheim, California, and Walt Disney
World, Lake Buena Vista, Florida

SELECTED BIBLIOGRAPHY

Brooklyn Botanic Garden, *Plants and Gardens
Handbook 36: Trained and Sculptured Plants,* first
published New York 1968.

Country Life, *Gardens in Edwardian England,*
reprinted Antique Collector's Club,
Woodbridge, 1985.

C. H. Curtis and W. Gibson, *The Book of Topiary,*
first published 1904, reprinted Tuttle, Tokyo, 1985.

W. Dallimore, *Holly, Yew and Box,* first published
1908, reprinted Minerva Press, 1978.

Michael A. Dirr, *Manual of Woody Landscape Plants,*
third edition, Stipes, Champaign, Illinois, 1983.

Paul Edwards, *English Garden Ornament,* Bell,
London, 1965.

Miles Hadfield, *Topiary and Ornamental Hedges,*
Black's, London, 1971.

Hillier's Manual of Trees and Shrubs, David and
Charles, Newton Abbot, fourth edition, 1972.

Edward Hyams, *English Cottage Gardens,* first
published London, 1970, reprinted Whittet, 1986.

A. D. C. Le Sueur, *The Care and Repair of Ornamental
Trees,* London, 1934.

Nathaniel Lloyd, *Craftsmanship in Yew and Box,*
Benn, London, 1925.

F. W. Shepherd, *RHS Wisley Handbook 17: Hedges
and Screens,* London, 1974.

Cecil Stewart, *Topiary, an Historical Diversion,*
Golden Cockerell Press, London, 1934.

INDEX

PICTURE CREDITS AND ACKNOWLEDGMENTS

Heather Angel/Biofotos: 23, 32, 41, 65
The Bridgeman Art Library: 14
Linda Burgess/Botanical Pictures: title page, 54
Robert César/Weidenfeld Picture Library: 19
Eric Crichton: 67
C.M. Dixon/Photo Resources: 13
Andreas Einsiedel: 16
Derek Fell: 36, 66, 76, 79 bottom, 83
The Garden Picture Library/Henk Dijkman: 60
John Glover: 6–7
Jerry Harpur: 94
Arthur Hellyer: 34
Marijke Heuff: 21, 31, 35, 75
Michael Holford: 12
Walter Hunnewell: 29
Andrew Lawson: 30, 42, 46, 87, 98
Georges Lévèque: 64
Longwood Gardens: 82
Tony Lord: 10, 97, 101
Tania Midgley: 37, 43, 44, 91
Tony Mott: 17
The National Trust/Nick Meers: 102
Nature Photographers: 77
Godfrey New/Royal Horticultural Society Library: 15, 18, 22, 25, 27, 72
Hugh Palmer: 79 top
The Parnham Trust: 48
Clay Perry: 74
Fritz von der Schulenburg: 58
Edwin Smith: 45, 49, 52
Harry Smith: 84
Sotheby's: 24
Jessica Strang: 28, 38, 39, 59, 63, 71
Dr Christopher Thacker: 20, 78
Michael Warren/Photos Horticultural: 50, 68, 99
Peter Woloszynski: 62

Photograph on page 26 by kind permission of the Marquess of
Tavistock and the Trustees of the Bedford Estates.

Colour illustrations by Liz Pepperel; line drawings by Graham Rosewarne

The author and publishers would also like to thank the
following people for their advice and assistance:
Tim Clevely for his sketches; Mrs. Lothian Lynas of New
York Botanic Garden; Ron Nettle; and Ernie
Wasson of Green Animals Garden.

ART CENTER COLLEGE OF DESIGN LIBRARY
1700 LIDA STREET
PASADENA, CALIFORNIA 91103